HEMP MASTERS GETTING KNOTTY:

Ancient Hippie Secrets for Knotting Hip Hemp Jewelry

SPRINGDALE PUBLIC LIBRARY
405 S. PLEASANT ST.
SPRINGDALE, AR 72764

T3-BPX-914

10/04

Written and Illustrated by
Max Lunger

Copyright @ XXIII by Eagle's View Publishing Company. All rights reserved.
No part of this book may be reproduced or transmitted by any form or by any means, electronic
or mechanical, including, but not restricted to, photocopying, recording or by any information
storgage and/or retrieval system without permission in written form from the publisher.

Eagle's View Publishing Company
A WestWind, Inc. Company
6756 North Fork Road
Liberty, UT 84310

Library of Congress Number: 2001012345
ISBN: 0-943604-62-1

First Edition

14 13 12 11 10 9 8 7 6 5 4 3 2

TABLE OF CONTENTS

ACKNOWLEDGMENTS

This second book of Ancient Hippie Secrets was also conceived by my Brother, Robert Johnson and I. Again we would like to thank all you beautiful people that have purchased the Hemp Masters Knotting Guides for you are the creators and the messengers of the re-growth of a hempen way of life in the US. Thanks for all that you do! Our Hero's!

There are many kind people that have helped in the process of creating this second book of Hemp Masters. For creative incentive: Herb Hempstead, Stan & Debbie Brennen, Lisa Winters and the many more kind people that asked those famous questions. Oh my God, how do you do that? And when is your second book coming out? Thank you so much! We also want to thank our publisher, Monte Smith, and the person most responsible for making this book what it is, our editor, Denise Knight.

We believe that you can be anything this time around. The true secret to life is to love all and be happy, for if you go through life looking for misery and despair, you will find what you seek. There is a good side to everything if you look hard enough. The Ancient Hippie Secret to Life is to live your life through your talents rather than your abilities. What a Concept!

For more information about hemp, please see our website at *www.hempmasters.com*.

May the Hemp Goddess always smile up on you and yours!

The Knotty Poem

You're sure to get knotty
Old hippie school style,
No trippen on trouble,
Just heavy on smile.

You know you've been knotty
If your fingers are sore,
When they dig your creations
Heavy bank you will score.

When they ask how you did it,
With bank and a smile,
Just say you got knotty,
Old hippie school style.

INTRODUCTION

We decided to take our second book to the extreme, so we tripped on just how knotty we could get. Some of the heavy patterns in this knotting guide are sure to put Dank Bank into any Hippies pocket. Our knotting guides are designed to help the novice and the professional hemp jewelry crafter through the process of creating heavy hemp jewelry and many other Dank Bank decorative pieces to dig on.

The Hemp Masters knotting guide is designed to help crafters through the process of creating hemp jewelry and other decorative pieces. Suggestions include bracelets, anklets, necklaces, chokers, car mirror charms, key chains, wall tapestries, plant hangers, speaker hangers, and hackysacks. These are just some of the possibilities. For gifts, or for profit, making hemp jewelry is a very rewarding craft.

Other mediums that are fun to use with the hemp masters knotting guide are jute, colored yarn, colored floss, horse hair, rope, leather strips, and even old clothing cut into strips.

Using Colored Hemp Twine

The concept of colors in hemp jewelry opened hundreds of visions for this hippie when considering intertwining these colors with all of the patterns in the first book. What a Bank Making Concept! If you made bank from the patterns in the first book, you are going to freak on the bank you'll score when adding color to your creations.

The most important thing to remember when using hemp cord or twine is to keep the strings twisted as the knots are tied. "Always be twisted while being knotty." Pay attention to the direction the hemp is twisted and always reinforce the twist in the hemp before the knots are tied tight. If you remember to do this, the jewelry will be defined and score much bank in a most heavy way.

Terms Used

Bunk (Hemp) - bad, not worthy; a section of cord where two lengths have been connected. A section like this is bunk because it usually has a knot which must be frayed out to make the jewelry look consistent (see Ancient Hippie Secrets and Helpful Hints).

Carrier or Bead Carrier - one or more cords which knots are tied around. Beads are also threaded onto these cords.

Cord versus Twine - cord and twine are wound in opposite directions when the fibers are spun. Cord is wound counter-clockwise and twine is wound in a clockwise direction.

Hip - the portion of a square knot created when the vertical cord passes over the two horizontal cords. Or a body part. Also someone loved by all.

Heavy - a reference to the weight or size of cords used in hemp jewelry, or of one's ex-mother-in-law. Profitable. Something that blows your mind.

Knotter - one or more cords used to tie a knot. Or a person in denial of their own actions (I did

1

not!). Not to be confused with Knottier, which is a naval rank.

Phish (Fish) Bone - a style of knotting heavy bank jewelry (just one of Hemp Masters' best)

Sinnet - a vertical chain or braid of repeated knots.

Style - type of jewelry. Or a hair cut. A hip line of clothing - to be in or out of style (who cares?).

Bank - $, money, folding stuff, lettuce, long green, script, bread.

Bummer - Not happy, a person that looks for the worst in everything, something that doesn't go the way you want, a vibe that really sucks. What a Bummer!

Dank - A term used to describe something of high quality or of superb taste. Wow, that's way dank!

Dig - to understand or like something (I dig it.). To understand or like someone (I dig you!). What the boss tells you if you are a dirt pilot.

Freak Out - when in trouble, when in doubt, run in circles, scream and shout; a bunk expression of human emotion.

Funky - a style of music; a hair cut; something unusual; a verbal description of anything that makes you go hmmm...(that's funky!).

Head - Someone who fondles too much hemp, that thing on top of your shoulders that should be used as much as possible, something a lot of people have lost or didn't know they had.

Hippie - a human being.

Jive - rhythmic speech, odd directions. Not to be confused with jive turkey.

Kind - You know, an expression of emotion, a good deed, to be kind, kind people hug, this is so kind! You so Kind, Got Kind? Can you dig kind?

Knotty - Get your mind out of the gutter: An expression from the soul of hemp masters, something that could make your fingers hurt. We are so Knotty!

Man - a slang word for the human species. Not to be confused with *The Man*.

Om - a mantric word (Hinduism). Om is where the heart is. There's no place like Om. Om my God! It's good to be Om. A man's Om is his castle. Welcome Om.

Score - to purchase or to find. To touch home plate; get a touchdown; make a goal; keep track of points in a card game. The art of competition (Hey Man, what's the score?).

Stash - a special supply of craft materials, a special place.

Trip - to go somewhere (take a trip); to think (trip on this); to think everyone is after you (wow, he's tripped out); not understanding how something works (that's trippy).

Truck on Down - walk, run or ride to a desired destination.

Vibe - Good or Bad, I feel the vibes, a sixth sense, a feeling you get from someone, something or somewhere. Can you dig those vibes?

Hemp Facts Everyone Should Know

Hemp has been around for hundreds of years, from ancient Egypt, to the birth of the United States of America, to the present day, and it has been used for many purposes. The U.S. Constitution, the Bill of Rights and many laws were written on hemp paper. The first pair of 501 jeans and the first U.S. flag were made from hemp.

The harvesting of hemp was deemed illegal in 1937. In 1941 Japan stopped all shipments of hemp into the United States and the U.S. government and industry changed their views on hemp (what a concept!). During World War II the U.S. government encouraged farmers to grow hemp because the navy needed rope. Every farmer in America had to sign a document stating that they had watched the government produced film called *Hemp for Victory*. Those who checked the yes box, along with their families, were exempted from the draft. Hemp, Hemp Hurrah! They had Hemp that day!

Webster's New World Dictionary defines hemp as follows: hemp (hemp), n. 1. a tall Asiatic plant of the nettle family, having tough fiber. 2. the fiber, used to make rope, sailcloth, etc. - hempen, adj. The fiber, of course, may be used to create beautiful jewelry and that's what this book is all about; teaching the reader the basics of knotting and design.

Hemp is considered by many to be the world's most versatile and valuable resource. It provides the raw material for more products (over 50,000) than any other plant. The stems are used to produce fabric, fuel, paper and other commercial products. The hemp is dried and broken down into two parts; thread-like fibers, and bits of "hurd" or pulp. From the fiber strands, which are spun into thread, come such products as the world's strongest natural fiber rope, and durable, high quality textiles of all types and textures. These fabrics can be made into sails, clothing, and fine linens. From the "hurd", which is 77% cellulose, come such products as tree-free, acid-free paper, non-toxic paints and sealants, industrial fabrication materials, construction materials, biodegradable plastics, and much, much more.

Hemp is also one of the best sources of plant pulp for biomass fuel to make natural gas, charcoal, methanol, gasoline, or even to produce electricity.

The hemp seed is used to produce nutritional oils, lubricants and fuels. Hemp seeds are also an excellent source of protein.

Hemp foliage has also been promoted for its medicinal value in easing pain, relieving stress and treating illnesses from glaucoma to nausea in AIDS and cancer patients. Hemp roots even play an important role by anchoring and invigorating the soil, providing erosion control and preventing mud slides.

Hemp is the only plant that grows up to 20 feet throughout the United States. One acre of hemp can replace five acres of cotton used for material; over 50% of the pesticides applied in the U.S. are used on cotton crops - less than 3% kills the insects, the rest goes into the ground water or is embedded in our clothing (what a concept!). One acre of hemp can replace four acres of trees used for paper; and hemp has a three month growing season! Hemp's abundant yield can add over a trillion dollars to the U.S. economy and assure us prosperity, plenty and economic stability. These facts are substantial and make the argument for legalization of the hemp industry in the United States ... a critical one. Just think, if we grow enough hemp and save enough trees, global warming could be a thing of the past, not to mention the national debt. Hemp can save our planet!

Gettin' Knotty

We like hemp, we think it's cool,
The longest natural fiber, is our tool,
It grows 20 feet, in 100 days,
So we can get knotty, in thousands of ways.

We tie hemp; this is true,
We'll tie hemp, just for you,
Our hands are strong, from knots pulled tight,
So our creations, will bring delight.

As you decide to work this craft,
Just use this book, as your staff,
As you begin to make your bank,
It's your creations you should thank.

We tie it simple or to extreme,
Ancient hippie secrets are on the scene,
Knowledge is king we believe,
So tell everyone what you conceive.

Happy hempen that's what we are,
The joy of creation will take you far,
If you feel we bent your brain,
Try writing this book, we feel the same.

BEGINNING

The hippest, most common, question asked is how long should the hemp be cut when beginning a piece. The answer is that it depends on the style, be it necklace, choker, anklet or bracelet. Say it is a necklace. Most necklaces measure 18 to 20 inches in length. The amount of hemp cord needed is two pieces, each approximately eight feet in length. Both cords will be folded in half, but not cut.

The following chart is a guide for 45 lb. test (approx. 2 mm) cord. The chart applies to jewelry with a consistent series of knotting throughout the pattern. Other factors will vary the length needed: The more inconsistent the knotting or the more beads included in the pattern, the less cord will be needed. The length of cord needed will also vary depending on the gauge (thickness) of cord used and on how tight the knots are pulled. The thinner the cord, the more knots will be tied for a given length of jewelry and the more cord will be needed. Tighter knots require less cord per knot, but more knots are needed to achieve a given length. Finally, it is always better to cut the cord too long and have some left over, than it is to cut the cord too short. Experience is the only solution (Ommm).

Style	Length of piece	Cut Length (2)	Folded Length (4)
Necklace	18 to 20 inches	8 feet	4 feet
Choker	13 to 18 inches	6 to 8 feet	3 to 4 feet
Anklet	9 to 13 inches	4 to 6 feet	2 to 3 feet
Bracelet	5 to 8 inches	3 to 4 feet	1.5 to 2 feet

To begin, cut two cords to the length needed for the style being made. Fold both cords in half. If any of the loop closures will be used, **do not cut** the cords (loop closures are used on nearly all the designs in this book). This gives four equal lengths of cord coming from the two

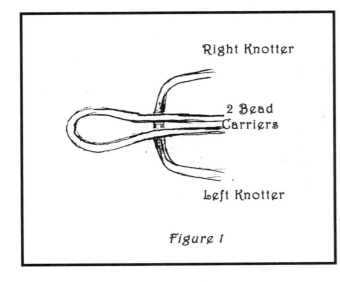

Right Knotter

2 Bead Carriers

Left Knotter

Figure 1

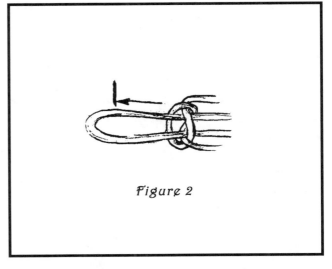

Figure 2

5

loops (folds) at the top (two from each fold). For example, to start a necklace, two cords each eight feet long, would be folded in half. This will result in four cords, each four feet in length, with two loops at the top.

Place one loop inside the other and hold the four cords so that they do not cross one another. It may be easier to pin the top (fold) of these cords to a craft board. The two cords from the inside loop should lie inside the two cords from the outside loop. The "outside" cords, on the left and right, are the *Knotters*; they will be the cords doing the work. The center two cords are the *Bead Carriers* or *Fillers*, around which the knots will be tied. The knotting cords will be referred to as *Right* and *Left* and are held in the right and left hand respectively (**Figure 1**). Note: The bead carrier cords do not have to be as long as the knotter cords **if the carriers will not be used for any knotting at any point** in the pattern. However, many designs use switch knots or require the carriers to be pulled out as knotters.

Pull the inside loop in front of and above the outside loop (see **Figure 1**).

With the right and left cords from the outside loop, tie a loose Half Knot around the cords from the inside loop (see **Figure 2**). Slide the half knot close to the end of the inside loop and pull this knot tight. (See **Page 11** for directions on tying a Half Knot, if needed.)

Congratulations! The Knotters (outside loop cords) and Carriers (inside loop cords) have just been established for this piece of hemp work. Any pattern of knots described in this book can now be tied. This is also the beginning of the Slide Loop Clasp, a Hemp Masters Original (see **Page 23**) and a few other good closures for hemp jewelry.

Another way to begin knotting is to use a button (any button will do) or a flat bead. If the button has four holes, the holes should be big enough to accommodate a single cord; if

the button has two holes, they must each accommodate two cords; if the button has only one hole it should accommodate four cords. If the holes are too small, *don't freak out*. There have been many devices invented that will correct this bunk hole (i.e. a file, sandpaper or saw).

The button will become the center of the pattern, with hemp knotted on either side. In this case, the two beginning cords should be cut after they are folded, resulting in four cords of equal length.

The button in the photographed example (**Page 7**) has four holes, but the beginning positions of the cords are the same, regardless of the number of holes. Thread the first two cords through the top two holes in the button, positioning the button in the center of the cords. (For a two hole button, thread these two cords through the top hole and for a one hole button, position them at the top of the single hole.) Fold the cords in half and to the top, catching the button in the loop this creates.

Thread the second two cords through the bottom two holes in the button and fold them in half to the bottom. (For a two hole button, thread these two cords through the bottom hole and for a one hole button, position them at the bottom of the single hole.) This gives four strands at the top of the button (two strands from each cord; one becomes a knotter on the outside and one becomes a carrier on the inside) and four strands at the bottom of the button (again, knotters on the outside and carriers on the inside). This is shown as **Step 1** in the first photograph.

Tie a Half Knot on either side of the button to secure the button and all the cords in position (see **Step 2** photo). Tie the same pattern on either side of the button and this piece of hemp jewelry will be done. The third photograph on **Page 7** shows the cords threaded through a single hole flat bead, with work begun on the first half of the piece.

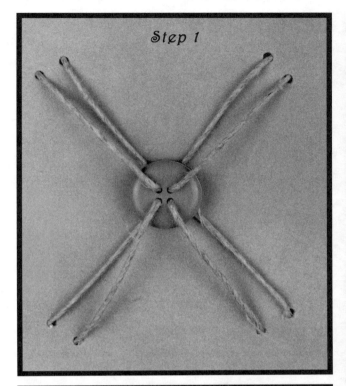

Step 1

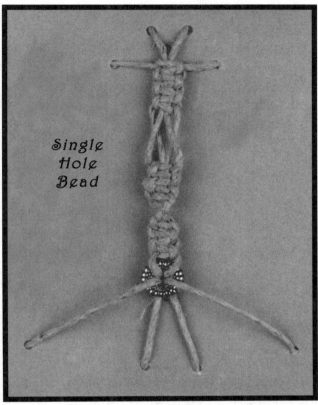

Single
Hole
Bead

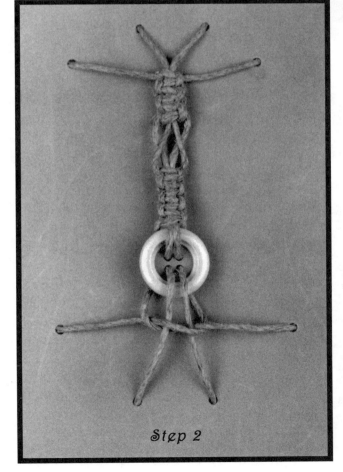

Step 2

Ancient Hippie Secrets and Helpful Hints

Buying Hemp - Notice the gauge or test weight of the hemp. The author's favorite sizes are 20 lb. (about 1mm), 45 lb. (1.5 to 2 mm) and 170 lb. (about 4 mm) test. Also available is 80 lb. test (about 3 mm). Also notice the clarity or how tight and clean the cord or twine is wound. If the cord is too fuzzy, beeswax is a great conditioner.

Growing Hemp - Don't do this in the USA (it is still illegal in most states)!

Colored Hemp - Colored hemp is made a bit fuzzy and weaker by the process used to dye it. Therefore, it works best if used in conjunction with stronger, naturally colored hemp. Use beeswax to eliminate the fuzziness and take care not to pull the colored hemp too hard, or it might break. If it does break, undo the last four or five knots and add a new colored piece.

Tying All Knots - Before pulling any knot tight, twist the hemp cord in the same direction that the cord is wound. This is important for maintaining the shape of the knot and helps define the more complicated patterns. This technique is especially helpful when using Alternating Square Knots, Butterfly Knots, Pretzel Knots or loops of any kind.

Adding Cords

Knotters Are Too Short - If the knotters get too short to finish a piece, *don't freak out.* Cut a piece of cord long enough to finish knotting the pattern; when deciding the length, keep in mind that this cord will be folded and become both knotters. This technique can also be used to add extra cords and hide them inside the knotting.

Place the middle of the cord to be added on top of and across the bead carriers. Pull the existing knotters over this new cord and tie a Half Knot around the bead carriers. Be sure to pull this half knot snug around the new cord being added; this knot hides the addition of the new cord and helps to secure it (see **Figure 3**).

Pinch the short, old knotters parallel to the bead carriers. Use the ends of the cord just added as the new knotters and tie a Square

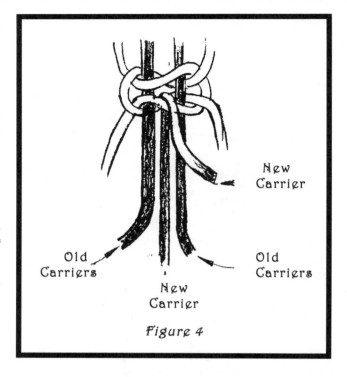

Figure 4

Knot around all four of the old cords - allow the short old knotters to become carriers for the time being. Tie at least three more tight Square Knots with the new knotters - this holds all the cords securely in place. Glue (not super glue) also helps. Cut off the old knotters below the square knots just tied.

Carriers Are Too Short/Need Another Carrier - If the carrier(s) get too short to finish a piece, *again, don't freak out.* One or more new carrier(s) can be added at the same time to replace the short ones. This technique can also be used to add an extra carrier. Cut one or more cords to the length needed.

Place the new cord next to the short carrier(s). Pull the cord to be added at least one inch above the last knot tied. With the knotters, tie a Half Knot around all the carriers, new and old. Take the one inch piece of new cord, which is above the knot, and fold it down over the half knot, so it lies next to the other bead carriers (see **Figure 4**). Tie three or more tight Square Knots to hold everything securely in place, then cut the short carrier(s). A small amount of glue on the carriers and

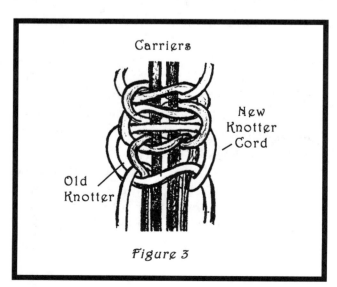

Figure 3

square knots will also help hold them in place.

One Knotter is Too Short - If only one knotter is too short, this too can be corrected. Simply add one new carrier as just described. Once the new cord is secured, bring the new cord out as a knotter. At the same time, bring the old short knotter to the center as a carrier until it runs out or is cut off.

Adding Extra Cords (A Masters Trick) - Some more advanced patterns require the addition of extra cords. For instance, this technique may be used to go from a single knotted portion to two connected portions which are the same thickness as the original as shown in the Rear View Mirror Charm on **Page 93**.

To add extra cords, lay them across the carriers and put the knotters on top of the cords being added. In the **photograph** the cords labeled 1, 2, and 3 are new and lie in front of the carriers. New cords can be added either in front of or behind the carriers. Tie a Half Knot tight against the added cords (**Step 1**), then tie three Square Knots to hold the added cords in

place. Leave the new cords out to the side or pinch them in with the carriers (**Step 2**) depending upon the pattern being tied. This technique is particularly useful for Phish Bone and Alternating Square Knot patterns.

Preventing Knot Slippage - This technique will stop knots and beads from slipping along the bead carriers. Tie a Half Knot with just the carriers, then use the knotters to tie a series of knots over the knot in the carriers.

Threading Small Beads - To get small beads to thread more easily on hemp cord, put some glue on the cut end and twist the cord as it dries. If the bead hole is very small, cut the end of the cord at an angle and twist the end into a point as the glue dries. Do not use super glue as it makes the hemp brittle and causes it to break. Rubber cement is the best score.

Bunk Hemp - No matter how good the roll looks, there will always be a "bunk" spot

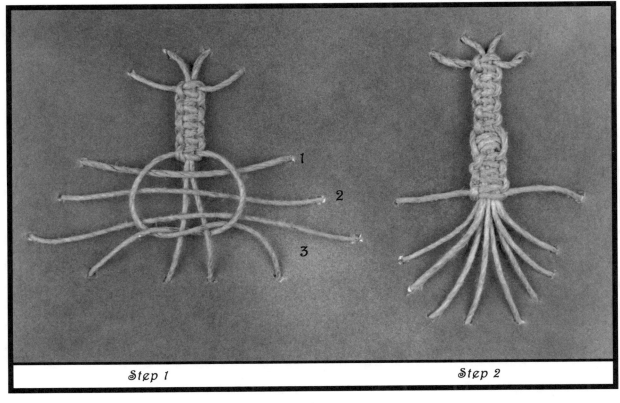

Step 1   Step 2

where the bead stops. To correct this headache spot, lick the hemp or get it wet and scratch it to make it fray. Then cut the frayed edges until the bead passes over the spot. Too much and the cord will break! Glue helps keep the cord wound.

Dirty Jewelry - Wash your hands! Or wash the jewelry using warm water, shampoo and conditioner. Air dry. Washing weakens hemp over time, but many people wear simple hemp jewelry patterns all the time, including in the shower. Complicated patterns do not fare as well when washed (see wet hemp), and this should be avoided.

Wet Hemp - Hemp swells when it is wet; the more exposure to water, the softer and weaker the hemp will be. Water and washing are not recommended for the more complicated patterns.

Selling Hemp Jewelry - Be aware that many people are ignorant of the history and the possibilities of hemp products. To sell at an established business, ask permission from the manager or owner first, they like that! To sell wholesale to a business, cut the retail price by 50%. If selling by consignment, be careful and keep good books. In the process of sales, always smile and acknowledge the praise received. Failure to do so means asking for it twice. To acknowledge rejection, just smile and say thank you.

There are two basic knots used to make hemp jewelry, the Half Knot and the Half Hitch. Both knots are attractive and functional, which is one reason for their popularity in hemp jewelry projects. The other reason is that there are many variations of these two knots, which allows the knotter dozens of choices for pattern combinations. There are many *funky* knots which can be used with hemp; the best are in this guide.

In addition, this section gives knots for beginning and creating clasps or closures for hemp jewelry. An abbreviation is given in parentheses for each knot, and this abbreviation, followed by a number, is used to indicate which knots, and how many, are needed in the patterns at the end of the book.

Unless otherwise indicated all these knots are illustrated with four parallel cords. This is done by starting with four separate cords or two cords folded at the center.

Be aware that more than two knotters and any number of bead carriers can be used to create different effects in hemp jewelry. The basic procedure for each knot remains the same as when using four cords.

Beads are often threaded on the bead carriers between knots, or they can be strung on all four cords between knots. Actually, beads can be added to any of the cords, or any combination of cords, in any position which pleases the jewelry maker.

Lark's Head (LH) Mounting Knot

This knot is most often used for mounting cords on rods and rings. It can also be used for connecting cords. Cut the cord lengths as instructed for the pattern. Mount

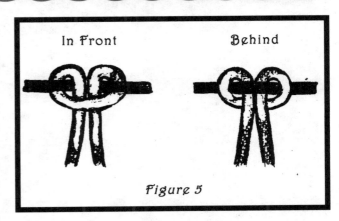

In Front   Behind

Figure 5

them one at a time, unless otherwise specified. Find the center of the cord and fold it in half. The Lark's Head knot may be done with the cord laying in front of or behind the rod or ring. Take the loop formed and wrap it over the top of the rod or ring. Bring both ends of the cord under the rod or ring and through the loop. Pull the loop snug (see **Figure 5**).

HALF KNOT AND ITS VARIATIONS

Half Knot (HK)

A Half Knot (HK) can be either right or left handed. If no direction is indicated in a pattern, use whichever is easiest.

Start a Right Half Knot (RHK), with the Right cord. Place it *over* the two center cords and *under* the Left cord. Let go of the Right cord and let it lay on the craft board (see **Step 1 Right** in photo on next page). Take the Left cord *under* the two center cords and *up through* the loop made by the Right cord. Take care that the center two carriers remain in their original position. Pull the outside cords taut (see **Step 2 Right** in photo on next page).

A Left Half Knot (LHK) is made using

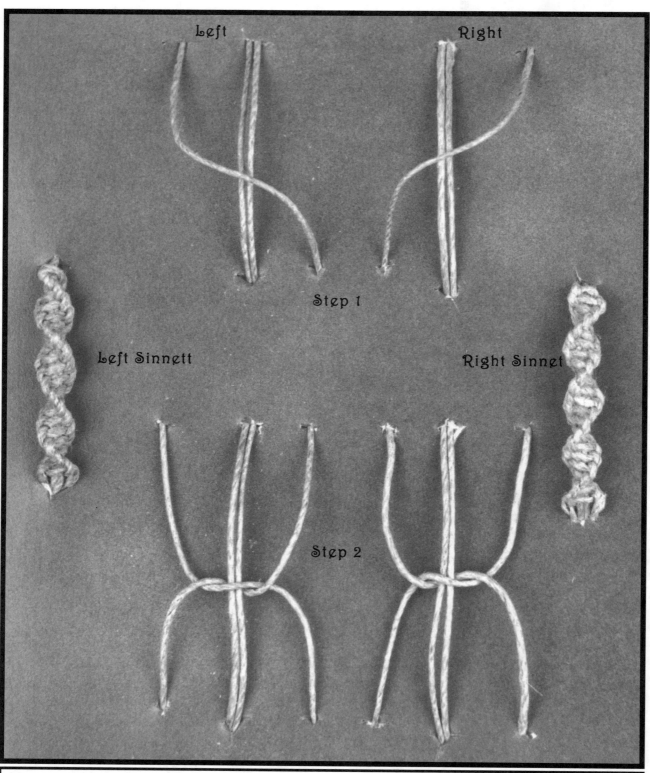

Left

Right

Step 1

Left Sinnett

Right Sinnet

Step 2

HALF KNOTS

the same procedure as for a Right Half Knot, only the knot is started with the Left cord, followed by the Right cord (see **Steps 1 and 2 Left** in photo).

Half Knot Sinnet (HKS)

A Sinnet is a vertical chain or braid of repeated knots. Using Half Knots creates a spiral braid. To make a Half Knot Sinnet, repeat Steps 1 and 2 of the Half Knot several times. Use either all Right Half Knots or all Left Half Knots. After the first few knots are completed, the Sinnet will start to twist; the direction of the twist depends on the type of Half Knot used. Allow the piece to twist, turning the work as the knotting progresses (see **Half Knot** photograph). The number of knots it takes to complete a full twist trips heavy (depends) on the thickness of cord being used. The thinner the cord, the sooner it twists and the more twists per inch.

Overhand Knot (OK)

An Overhand Knot (OK) is actually just a Half Knot tied in a single cord. To tie this knot, simply make a loop near the end of the cord. Bring the end around the cord and through the loop, as shown in the photo-

graph at left bottom. Pull the end to tighten the knot; move the loop to position the knot as it is tightened.

Square Knot (SK)

The Square Knot consists of two Half Knots, one Right and one Left. Square Knots can be either right or left handed, depending on which type of Half Knot is tied first. When a Square Knot (SK) is indicated in a pattern without a right or left designation, use whichever is easiest to tie (see **Figure 6**).

Start a Right Square Knot (RSK) by completing Steps 1 and 2 for a Right Half Knot (see **Page 12**). With steps 1 and 2 done, and the four cords laying side by side on the board, take the Left cord and place it *over* the two center carriers and *under* the Right cord. Let go of the Left cord and let it lay on the board (see **Step 3**).

Take the Right cord *under* the two center carriers and up through the loop made by the Left cord (see **Step 4**). Pull the knotting ends taut.

Note that when square knotting is started with the right cord *over* the carriers, the completed knot will have the "hip" (the vertical cord that passes over the two horizontal cords in the knot) on the right side of the knot (see **Finished Knot**).

A Left Square Knot (LSK), illustrated in **Figure 7** is done in the same manner as a Right

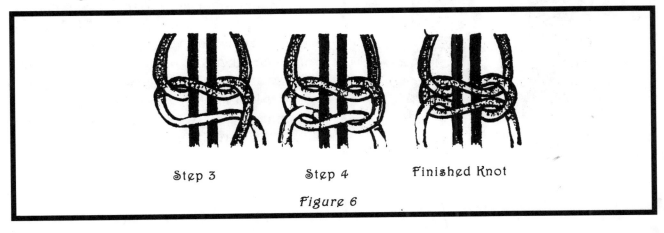

Step 3   Step 4   Finished Knot

Figure 6

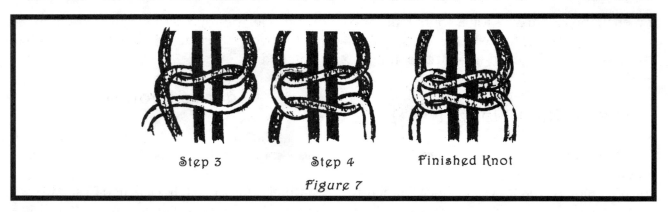

Step 3   Step 4   Finished Knot

Figure 7

Square Knot, except that it is begun on the left side with the Left cord. Start by completing Steps 1 and 2 for a Left Half Knot (see **Page 12**). Then take the Right cord and place it *over* the two center carriers and *under* the Left cord (see **Step 3**).

Take the Left cord *under* the two center carriers and up through the loop made by the Right cord (see **Step 4**). Since the knotting is started with the Left cord *over* the carriers, the completed knot will have the "hip" on the left side of the knot (see **Finished Knot**).

Remember, in the Square Knot the same cord always crosses over the top of the carri-

ers. When the four steps of the Square Knot are completed, the hip is on the same side as the cord used to start the knot.

Square Knot Sinnet (SKS)

To tie a Square Knot Sinnet, tie a series of Square Knots. Use all Right Square Knots to create a Right Square Knot Sinnet (RSKS) or all Left Square Knots to create a Left Square Knot Sinnet (LSKS). A Square Knot Sinnet lays flat. To determine how many Square Knots have been tied, count the hips on the side from which the knotting was started. In **Figure 8** there are five hips and therefor five knots in each sinnet.

Switch Knot (Switch)

The Switch Knot (Switch) is a hemp saver, it looks great in hemp jewelry, and it is easy to tie. To accomplish the Switch Knot, use two knotters and two carriers. Begin by putting the old knotters in front of and in between the two old carriers. Pull the old carriers away from each other and use them to tie a Square Knot around the old knotters, about 3/4" away from the last knot tied (see **Figure 9**). Now the old carriers are the new knotters and the old knotters are the new carriers.

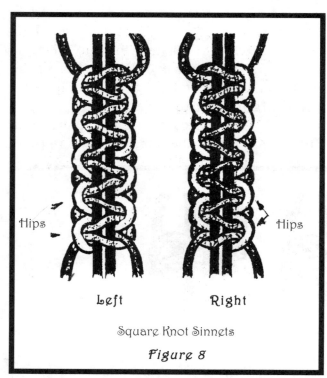

Hips   Hips

Left   Right

Square Knot Sinnets

Figure 8

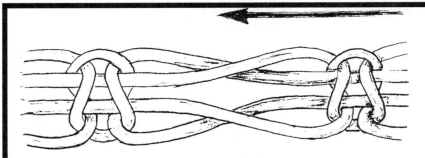

Figure 9

Switch Knot between sections of Square Knot Sinnet

Alternating Square Knot (ASK)

Dig This! The Alternating Square Knot (ASK) is tied using multiple sets of four cords each. The result is an attractive basket-weave pattern. Start by pinning the sets of four parallel cords next to one another on the craft board. The example in the photograph on **Page 16** is exploded for clarity and uses three sets of cords, but any number may be used.

Tie a Square Knot in each set of cords; these knots should be side by side, in the same place on each set of cords (see **Row 1** in the photo).

Momentarily set aside the two outside cords from both the right and left hand knots. Use the two inside cords from the right hand knot and the two right hand cords from the middle knot to tie a Square Knot. Use the two left hand cords from the middle knot and the two inside cords from the left hand knot to tie a second Square Knot (see **Row 2**).

Place all the cords in their original positions, as at the beginning of Row 1. For Row

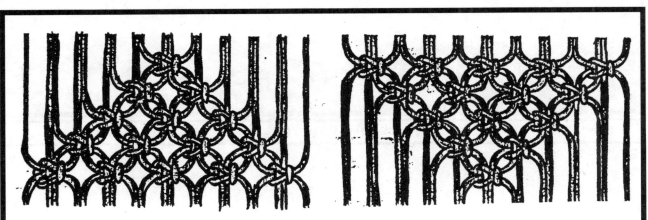

Increasing by one ASK per row   Decreasing by one ASK per row

Figure 10

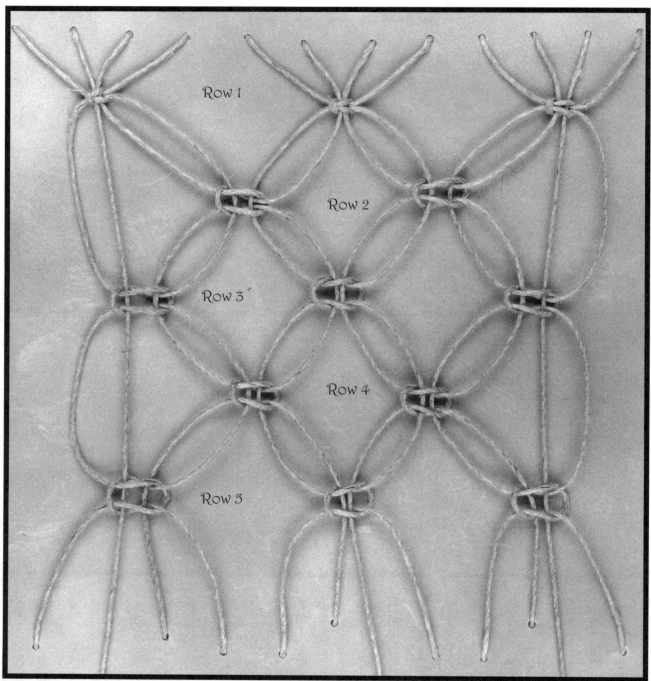

Row 1

Row 2

Row 3

Row 4

Row 5

Alternating Square Knot

3 tie a Square Knot in the left, middle, and right hand sets of cords, as was done in Row 1 (see **Row 3**). Row 4 is tied in the same way as Row 2, and so the pattern is established. Continue in this manner for as long as desired. Try allowing more or less space between the rows for different effects.

Many variations of the Alternating Square Knot are possible. **Figure 10** shows two of these. The first drawing shows increasing the number of Alternating Square Knots in each row by one (in a multiple set of cords). The second drawing shows the opposite effect, created by decreasing the number of Alternating Square Knots in each row by one.

Square Knot Button (SKB)

The Square Knot Button (SKB) is illustrated in the accompanying photographs (**Right**). Begin by leaving a small space where the button will be, looping the knotters just enough to allow the carriers to be threaded through the loops (see **Step 1**). Then tie three Square Knots (or more if a larger button is desired).

Take the center carriers and pull them *forward* and *up* to the space above the first Square Knot tied. Thread the carriers through the small loops created in Step 1, from *front to back*, and bring them down the back side of the Square Knot series (see **Step 2**). If a button is desired on the back side of the piece, just thread the carriers from back to front during Step 2.

From the back side, pull the carriers until the last knot tied is snug against the small space created in Step 1 (see **Step 3**). The series of three Square Knots originally tied will

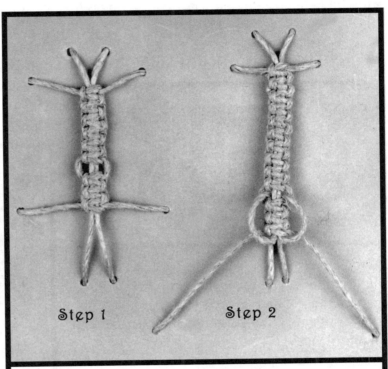

Step 1   Step 2

Square Knot Button

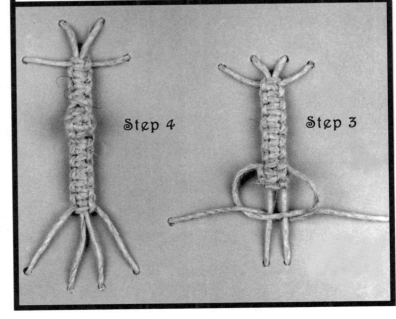

Step 4   Step 3

now be rolled into a Button. Secure the Button in position by tying another Square Knot directly below the roll. Continue knotting if desired (see **Step 4**).

This is a great method for ending and provides a button for the beginning loop or clasp to go around. The jewelry can be made adjustable in size by using more than one button.

Gathering Knot (GK)

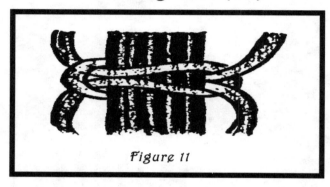

Figure 11

A Gathering Knot (GK) is one or more Square Knots tied around any number of cords to draw the group of cords together (see **Figure 11**). It may be used within a pattern or as a finishing step.

Butterfly or Picot Knot (BK)

A Picot or Butterfly Knot (BK) is illustrated in **Figure 12**. It consists of two Square Knots, tied at a distance from one another and then drawn together. Tie the first Square Knot in the regular manner. Tie the second Square Knot a half inch (or more) below the first knot (see **Step 1**). Hold the carriers firmly and gently slide the second Square Knot up into position below the first knot (see **Step 2**). The knotter cords between the two knots form loops as the knots slide together, resembling picot edging or butterfly wings.

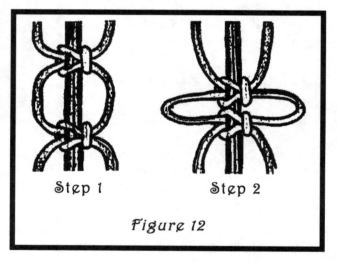

Step 1   Step 2

Figure 12

HALF HITCH AND ITS VARIATIONS

The most important thing to remember about Half Hitch Knots is that the Anchor Cord or Bead Carrier must be placed *on top* of the Knotter Cord before the knotting begins. Also remember that the Anchor Cord must be held taut as the knot is tied or the Half Hitch will not form properly. Half Hitches can be tied with the Anchor Cord in a horizontal, vertical, or diagonal position. In patterns, the first two letters of the abbreviation will specify the position of the Anchor Cord.

Half Hitch (HH)

To make a Half Hitch (HH), start with the Bead Carrier or Anchor Cord (A) *on top* of the Knotter Cord (K). Hold the Anchor (A) taut and take the Knotter (K) *over* the Anchor. Then take the Knotter *under* the Anchor and *up* through the loop formed by the Knotter around the Anchor (so that the Knotter crosses over itself; see **Figure 13**).

Note: A single Half Hitch tied in this manner only remains in position when there is tension on both ends of the Knotter, therefore it must be used in concert with other knots tied above and below the Half Hitch. To create a single Half Hitch which tightens on itself, go over the Anchor and *behind* the Knotter, before bringing the Knotter under the Anchor and through the loop (see photograph below).

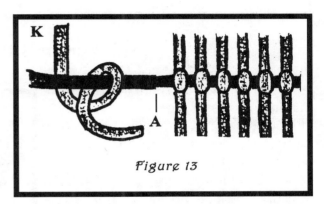

Figure 13

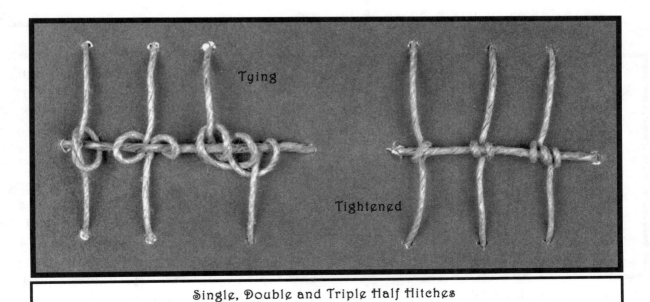

Tying

Tightened

Single, Double and Triple Half Hitches

Double Half Hitch (DHH)

Two Half Hitches tied around a Carrier or Anchor Cord creates a Double Half Hitch

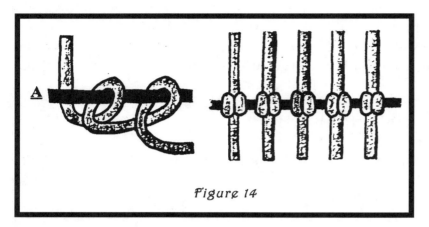

Figure 14

(DHH; see **Figure 14**). This is the most common way in which Half Hitches are tied. When completed, the Knotter cord will be positioned between the two Half Hitches and the knot is self-tightening. When attaching more than one knotter to an anchor cord, start with the first cord to the right of the anchor and continue left, one cord at a time, until all the desired cords have been tied around the anchor.

Other Half Hitch Variations

A Triple Half Hitch (THH), consisting of three consecutive Half Hitches (as the name implies) can also be tied around an anchoring cord, as shown in **Figure 15**.

Double or Triple Half Hitches can also be tied on an anchor cord which is running diagonally (see **Figure 16**).

A Half Hitch Sinnet (HHS) can be created by tying a series of Half

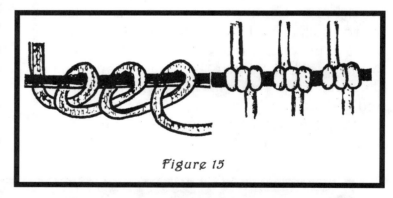

Figure 15

Hitches around a vertical anchoring cord. The sinnet can be either right-handed, with the loops on the right, or left-handed, with the loops on the left (see top left photograph on **Page 21**). More than one anchoring or carrier cord can be used depending on the number of cords being used in the project.

A different look can be achieved by switching the knotter and anchor cords between each Half Hitch tied. This is called an

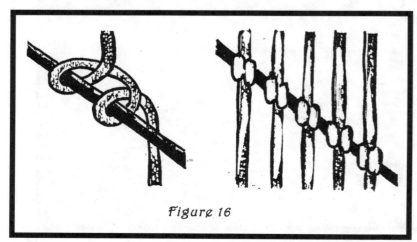

Figure 16

Alternating Half Hitch (AHH). This knot can be used to split a four cord piece into two halves, and is very attractive when tied with single cords and left spaced apart for an airy look, as in the

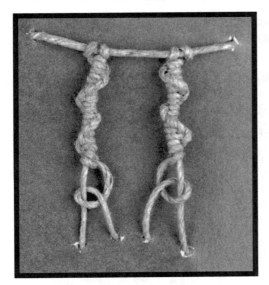

**Half Hitch Sinnets
Mounted with
Lark's Head Knots**

top right photograph on this page.

The Alternating Half Hitch can also be tied with double cords, if the artist does not wish to split the work into two halves. Still another variation is created by using first one Knotter and then the other to tie Half Hitches around the Carriers.

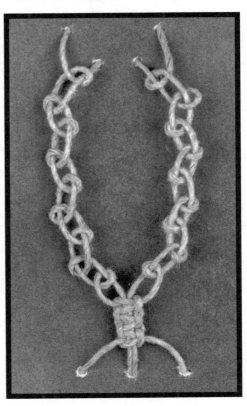

Alternating Half Hitch

STARTING AND FINISHING TECHNIQUES

Many types of closures are possible on necklaces, bracelets, and anklets. Most of them can be used on either end of the jewelry. Experiment a bit to find a favorite, as well as the type that best suits a particular project.

The easiest way to wear a piece of hemp jewelry is to leave some extra cord on the ends and tie them together with a Square Knot; however this should only be used if the jewelry will be worn until it falls off.

An Overhand Knot, tied using all four cords as a single cord, can be used to start or finish a piece of jewelry. A dab of glue will help hold it in place.

Square Knot

Finishing or Starting Wrap (W)

Overhand Knot

This technique, illustrated in **Figure 17**, can be used to begin or end a piece of hemp jewelry. A three inch wrap requires a separate cord approximately two feet in length. To begin, lay the extra cord along side (parallel to) the cords to be wrapped. Form a loop at the top which goes to the bottom of the area to be wrapped (see **Step 1**). Take one end of the extra cord (marked **B**) and wrap from the **bottom up** as many times as

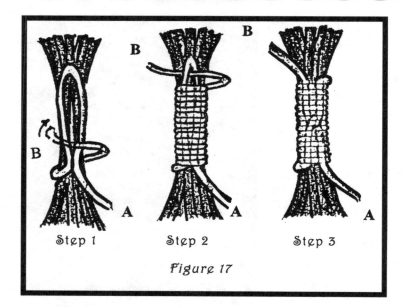

Step 1   Step 2   Step 3

Figure 17

desired, **pulling taut with each wrap.**

Take end **"B"** through the loop and hold it taught (see **Step 2**). Now pull on the other end of the extra cord (marked **A**) to bury the loop inside the wrap (see **Step 3**). **Do not** pull the end all the way through! Trim both ends close to the wrap. A bit of glue on the ends will help.

Loop Closures (LC)

These are a good starting point; first choose a bead or knot for the other end and then be sure to make a loop that the bead or knot can **just barely** pass through. For a Loop Closure at the start, begin with two looped cords, as indicated at the beginning of this Knotting Guide. Use the outside loop to tie a Square Knot (or any other knot desired in the pattern) around the inside loop, making sure that the end loop is the proper size (see **Figure 18**).

For a Loop Closure at the end of a knotted piece, tie off the knotters. Leave enough space for a loop along the carriers and then

Figure 18

tie an Overhand Knot using both carriers as a single cord (see **Figure 19**). Cut off any remaining cords and glue all ending knots and cuts. Another way to create a loop on the end (or at the beginning for that matter) is to leave enough space along all four cords, then tie a few more knots before ending. Split the cords, two to each side, and pass the bead or knot between them.

For an adjustable loop closure at the

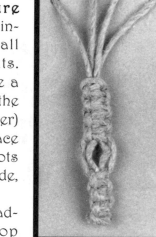

Loop Closures

Figure 19

start, make the loop larger and then slide a snug fitting bead over the loop and down to the knot (see **Figure 20**). When the loop is hooked around the opposite end of the piece, slide the bead along the loop to secure the closure.

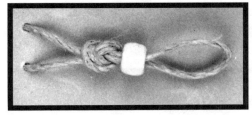

Adjustable
Loop
Closure

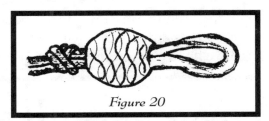

Figure 20

Slide Loop Clasp (SLC)

This is a Hemp Master's original clasp which creates a beginning loop whose size is adjustable. It is the author's favorite way of beginning a piece. Start with two looped cords, one inside the other, as indicated in the Beginning section of this book. Use the outside loop to tie a Square Knot around the inside loop. Leave just enough of the inside loop at the top to fit over the width of the piece; remember, this slide is adjustable, so the loop does not have to fit over the knot or bead at the other end.

Continue tying four or five square knots, until there is enough to hold comfortably (about

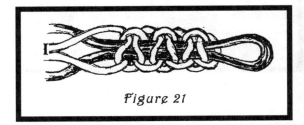

Figure 21

Slide Loop Clasp

a thumb width; see photograph). Then
Switch the knotters for the carriers (see **Figure 21**). About 3/4" below the last square knot, tie three Square Knots with the old carriers (around the old knotters). With the new carriers, tie a Half Knot snug against the last square knot. Continue tying Square Knots over the knot in the carriers. This will prevent knot slippage below the Switch.

To adjust the loop, grab the end of the loop with one hand and the section of square knots between the thumb and forefinger of the other hand. Slide the square knots down the carriers in the switch knot. The knotters will flare out to the sides. The square knots will stay at any point on the carriers, but the half hitch will ultimately stop their slide.

Bead Closures (BC)

Bead Closures are a good way to start or finish a pattern. Single or multiple beads can be strung on the starting loops before the knotting begins (see **Figure 22**). To create the same effect at the finish of a piece, cut one of the carriers and string the beads on the remaining carrier. Bring the end of the remaining carrier back up to the last knot tied, forming a loop. Secure the ends of the loop by tying 3 or 4 knots with the knotters. Cut and glue the ends of the knotters to finish the piece.

For a bead catch at the end of a pattern, tie off and glue the

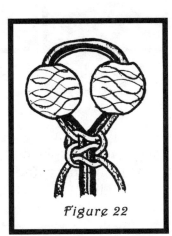

Figure 22

knotters. Then string the chosen bead(s) on the carriers and tie an Overhand Knot using both carriers as a single cord. Glue the knot (see **Figure 23** and left photograph). Another way to create a bead closure on either end is to "tie in" the bead (s). First string a bead on the carriers.

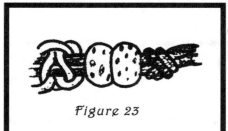

Figure 23

Then bring the knotters around either side of the bead and tie another knot. The photograph on the right shows two beads strung on the starting loop and a "tied in" bead which could be on either end.

Many variations are possible. For instance, crossing the carriers through a bead will

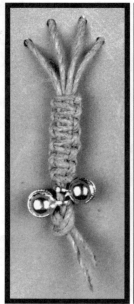
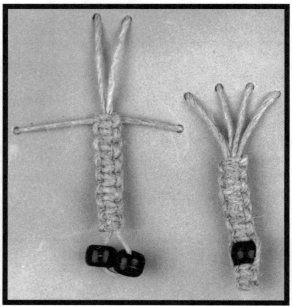

Bead Closures

Sideways Bead **Button End**

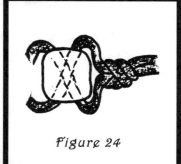

Figure 24

change the way it lies (see **Figure 24** and photograph on left). Or, if the beads are big enough, all four cords can be threaded through and then tied off. Buttons can also be used. Simply thread one or two carriers through the holes (two or four holes works best) and tie a knot on the back side of the button. Cut the carriers and glue the cut ends. Tie a knot over the cut ends, cut the knotters and apply more glue (see photograph on the right).

Ending Knots

To make a T-shaped end to fit through a loop, cut and glue the carriers, then take each knotter individually and tie an Overhand Knot on either side of the piece, snug against the sides of the last Square Knot (glue helps).

Adjustable sizing can be created by tying Overhand Knots to the side, without cutting the carriers, before the end of the piece. An end with T hooks such as these is called a Knuckled End (See photographs on next page).

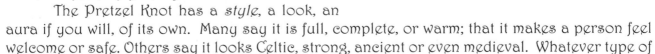

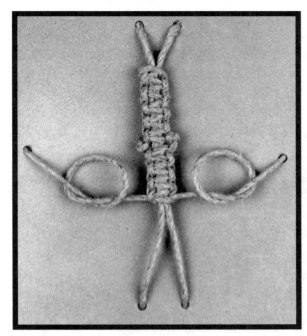

Tying T Hooks

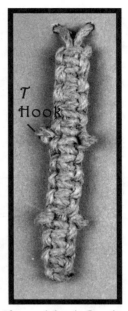

T Hook

Knuckled End

To create a "bump" for a loop to catch on, tie a Half Knot on *top* of the last knot tied, then tie a few more knots before ending the piece. This technique can also be used to create adjustable sizing by tying Half Knots on top of the pattern at spaced intervals from the end of the piece. An end with "bumps" such as these is called a Ripple End.

A simple way to end a piece of hemp jewelry is to cut the two middle carriers and put some glue on the cut ends. With the knotters, tie a tight Half Knot over the glued ends, then cut off the knotters. This ending technique is shown on the knuckled end pictured above.

To make a larger ending knot (End), which can be fastened through a loop, tie the knotters back over the end of the pattern. Use the same knots as were used on the end of the pattern. Glue the last knot and cut off the knotters. This ending technique is one of the author's favorites and is pictured on many of the project pieces in the next section.

KNOTS FOR MASTERS

Pretzel Knot (PK)

This knot is very seldom used by the new generation of hemp artists, but it may still look familiar (déja vu). The Pretzel Knot (PK) has been used in the U.S. as a decoration on military uniforms from the 1800's to the present day. It is also seen in the decorative weaves of modern baskets, macramé, door mats and rugs. And of course, Hemp Masters artists know how to use this knot in their hip, hemp jewelry.

The Pretzel Knot has a *style*, a look, an aura if you will, of its own. Many say it is full, complete, or warm; that it makes a person feel welcome or safe. Others say it looks Celtic, strong, ancient or even medieval. Whatever type of

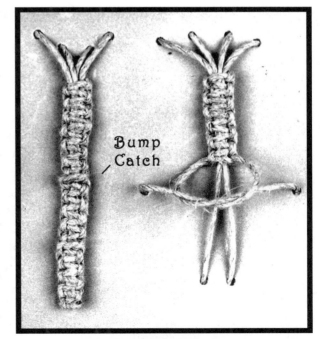

Bump Catch

Rippled End

jive they put on this *trippy hippie hemp twist*, it shows unique balance, for its grace is complete and defined. It is admired by all who see it.

Remember the following when tying a Pretzel Knot: This knot can be achieved with two, four, or any multiple of two cords. The photographs that illustrate these instructions show the structure of the Pretzel Knot with four

always faces the opposite set of cords (or the center of the piece, whichever is easier to visualize). Make a loop with one of the sets of cords; in the example the left set has been used to make the starting loop (see **Step 1**). Notice that the left set of cords crosses over (in front of) itself and that the loop is facing the right set of cords (towards the center). Hold the loop

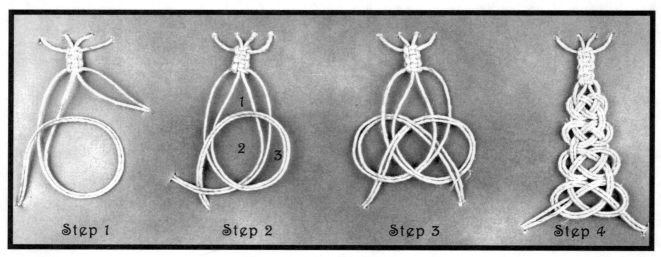

Step 1   Step 2   Step 3   Step 4

Tying a Pretzel Knot

cords, but feel free to use six or eight cords. **Be sure all cords remain parallel** to each other, through the entire knot, as the pretzel knot is carefully tightened. If more than one of these knots is tied in sequence, **each subsequent knot must start on the opposite side from the previous knot tied.** This will prevent the pattern from twisting.

The example which accompanies these instructions begins at the end of a square knot sequence, but it could be at the end of any sequence of knots. To start, split the cords at the end of the knotting sequence in half. In the example, the left knotter and left carrier are pulled to the left (the "left set") and the right knotter and right carrier are pulled to the right (the "right set").

Begin this knot on either side, just be sure that the starting loop always crosses over or in front of itself (just once) and that the loop

in the left thumb and forefinger, at the point where the left set of cords crosses itself.

With the right hand, bring the right set of cords **behind the starting loop,** so that it divides the loop in half, from top to bottom (see **Step 2**). With the right thumb and forefinger, hold the knot at the top of the loop, where the right set of cords crosses behind the top of the loop. Let go of the pattern with the left hand.

Follow the right set of cords down to about five or six inches below the big loop and, with the left hand, fold this set of cords to create a point or hemp needle. This will make it easier to weave the right set of cords through the loops created thus far. Make sure the right set of cords is over, or in front of, the left set of cords that lay below the big loop they were used to create (see **Step 2**). (*Hey man, don't freak out, get a grip and read it again.*)

Notice that there are now three half

loops. Above the big loop is a half loop created by the right and left sets of cord (Hole 1), and the big loop is divided into two half loops, top (Hole 2) and bottom (Hole 3).

With the hemp needle in the left hand, place the right set of cords behind the top left side of the knot and up through the top half loop (Hole 1). Then go over the top of the big loop and down into the middle half loop (Hole 2). Continue behind the right set of cords that divides the big loop in half and bring the hemp needle up through the bottom half loop (Hole 3). This is shown completed, but not tightened, in **Step 3**. The weaving is now finished, so release the fold of the hemp needle and pull the right set of cords out of Hole 3.

Make sure all cords in each set are parallel to one another before pulling the knot tight. Pull on the two sets of cords (left and right) and the Pretzel knot will begin to shrink and take shape. To position the Pretzel Knot at the desired point in the pattern, pull on the bottom right and left loops of the knot. Repeat this process until the knot is in the proper position and is the size desired (see **Step 4**).

Finished Hemp Jewelry Pieces Containing Pretzel Knots

Phish Bone (PB)

This knotting sequence takes a while to form its pattern. It can be tied with any number of knotter sets, but only one, lighter weight carrier is used. The more knotters, the wider the piece and the longer it takes for the pattern to form.

Setting up the cords for this knotting sequence is a very flexible process and depends on the vision of the artist. The carrier can be included at the beginning of the piece or it can be added at any point along the way. All the knotters can be added at once, or they can be added at a distance from one another. While tying this pattern, keep a tight twist in all the cords to maintain the definition of the Phish

Bone pattern. Beads can be added at any point in the Phish Bone; they have been used in this example to show how much panache they can add to a piece of hemp jewelry.

The photographs that illustrate these instructions start with a standard two knotter, two carrier setup, in which a Square Knot Sinnet has been tied. To set up for the Phish Bone, this is converted to three sets of knotters (all 45 lb. test) and a single 20 lb. test carrier. This example set up is just one of many possibilities.

The first step is the addition of the 20 lb. carrier. Adding a carrier is illustrated in the Ancient Hippie Secrets and Helpful Hints section (see **Page 8**). Cut the new carrier to the same length as the original carriers. Place the new cord parallel (next) to the existing carriers. Pull the top of the new cord about two inches above the last knot tied. With the knotters, tie a Half Knot around all three carriers. Take the two inch section of the new cord and fold it down over the Half Knot just tied, so it lies parallel to the other carriers. With the knotters, tie another Half Knot (the second half of a Square Knot) around the four carriers (see

There are now three sets of knotters (1, 2, & 3 from top to bottom) and one bead carrier. Place the #1 knotters in front of the other two sets and tie a Square Knot tight, just below the #3 knotters. Leave the #1 knotters to either side. Now place the #2 knotters in front of the #3 and the #1 knotters (beside the knot just tied) and tie a Square Knot tight, just below the #1 knotters. Leave the #2 knotters to either side

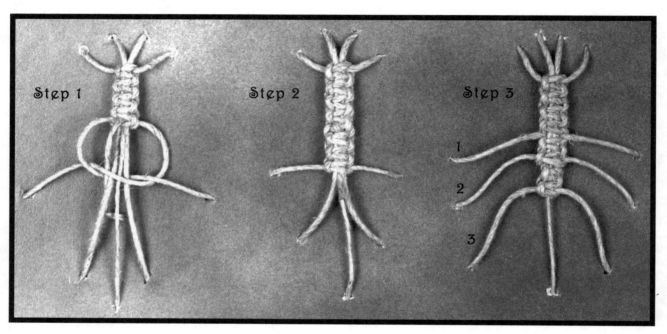

Setting Up for Tying the Phish Bone Pattern

Step 1). Tie three more Square Knots over all four carriers to hold everything securely in place (see **Step 2**). Cut the short (2") carrier if necessary.

Next add a new 45 lb. cord. Simply place the center of the new cord across (at right angles to) the carriers. Place the original knotters over the new cord and tie two Square Knots (see Adding Extra Cords, **Page 9**). Leave the new cord sticking out either side of the piece. To finish the set up, leave the original knotters to either side and tie two Square Knots with the two 45 lb. carriers. Leave these to either side as a third set of knotters (see **Step 3**).

of the piece. Place the #3 knotters in front of the #1 and #2 knotters and tie a Square Knot tight. Leave the #3 knotters to either side. **Be very aware of the size of the loops made by the knotters;** they should be either the same size throughout the pattern or each loop can gradually increase in size to the center point and then gradually decrease on the far side of the center point.

String a bead on the carrier and slide it up to the knot just tied. Place the #1 knotters in front of the #2 and #3 knotters and tie a Square Knot just below the bead (see **Step 4**). Slide everything snug and adjust the size of the knotter loops before the final tightening of

28

the knot below the bead.

Repeat this knotting sequence until the center point of the choker, bracelet, anklet, whatever, is reached (the second knot has already been tied with the #1 knotters, so start with the #2 knotters). String a center bead onto the bead carrier and snug it against the last knot tied

Hey man, remember to check the size of the piece against your body to establish where the center bead should be placed. This technique also helps in deciding on other bead placements when creating an original Fish Bone pattern.

To create the center point of the pattern, take the set of knotters **closest** to the center bead, go around either side of the center bead and tie a Square Knot tight against the other side of the center bead. Flip or rotate the entire piece over or

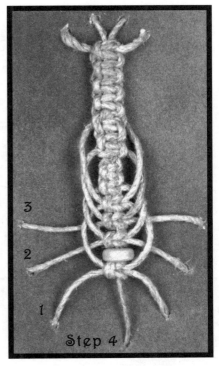

Tying the Phish Bone Pattern

face down (depending on your state of mind); this is labeled a **Flip** on the patterns. Using the next set of knotters above the center bead, pull them around the center bead and in front of the knotters just tied. Check the size of the loop and tie another tight Square Knot. Repeat this process with the third set of knotters. To complete the center point of the Phish Bone Pattern, bring the knotters closest to the center bead **in front of** the other two sets of knotters and tie a Square Knot.

Begin tying the second half of the Phish Bone pattern using the same knotting sequence given for the first half. The knotting and beading sequence from the center point to the end of the Phish Bone pattern must exactly match the knotting and beading sequence from the center point to the beginning of the Phish Bone pattern to give the jewelry balance. While it is not absolutely necessary to tie a center point, it certainly adds to the overall appearance of the pattern and your *bank*.

After the Phish Bone knotting sequence is completed, the extra cords must be secured and then cut so that the Square Knot Sinnet from the beginning of the piece can be repeated. To do this place all the cords, except the last set of knotters used, next (parallel) to the bead carrier. Use the remaining set of knotters to tie a Gathering Knot (use three square knots) tightly around all of the cords gathered in the center. Leave two of the

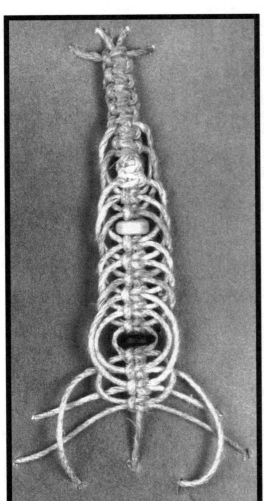

Center of Phish Bone Pattern Completed

heavier cords in the center to serve as carriers and cut the remaining center cords about 1/4 inch from the last knot tied. Apply some glue to the cut ends so that they will not slip. Tie a Square Knot Sinnet until this groovy creation is the desired length. This is one of the *coolest, bank maker,* patterns ever!

OVERHAND BRAID (BRAID)

Braids can be tied with either three or four cords. For a three-cord braid place the cords parallel to one another (see picture 1). The basic technique is to bring first the right cord and then the left cord over whatever cord is in the middle. Here is a step-by-step explanation of the first two sequences: Bring the right cord (#1) over the middle cord (#2), then bring the left cord (#3) over cord #1 (now in the middle). Now bring cord #2 over cord #3 (now in the middle). This sequence leaves the middle cord (#2) back in the middle, the original right cord (#1) on the left, and the original left cord (#3) on the right. To continue, bring cord #1 (from the left) over the middle cord (#2), then bring cord #3 (from the right) cord #1 (now in the middle). Repeat this sequence until the desired length of braid is reached. Just take it one step at a time and your creation will look so fine!

The four-cord braid is very attractive when made with cords of different colors. Place the cords parallel to one another (see picture 2). To start, weave the right cord over, under and over the other three cords and then weave the left cord under, over and under the other three cords.

Once this is done, continue the braid by weaving whatever cord is on the left under, over and under the other three cords. Here is a step-by-step explanation of the first sequence: To begin, weave the right cord (#1) from right to left (a in Picture 2); go over the first middle cord (#2), under the second middle cord (#3) and over the left hand cord (#4). Next, weave the left hand cord (#4) from left to right (b in Picture 2). It is already under cord #1 but make sure it is headed towards the right. Continue by weaving cord (#4) over cord #3, and

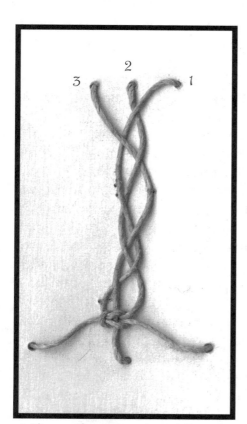

1. Three Cord Overhand Braid

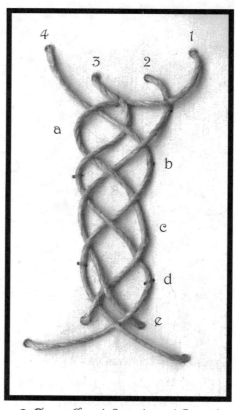

2. Four Cord Overhand Braid

under cord #2. Cord #1 is now on the left and must be woven towards the right (c in Picture 2). Go under cord #3, over cord #2, and under cord #4. This leaves cord #3 on the left, ready to weave towards the right (d in Picture 2). Go under cord #2, over cord #4, and under cord #1. Cord #2 is now on the left (e in Picture 2). Weave it right, going under cord #4, over cord #1 and under cord #3. This leaves cord #4 on the left. Repeat steps b through e until the braid is the length desired. This is more complicated than a three-cord braid, but not that difficult if taken one step at a time.

Hempen!

I know some knots with Optic Manipulation
So Dig on this, with Heavy Meditation.

They're Groovy, they're Cool,
They're one of a kind,
The coolest of knots,
They blow everyone's mind.

Be strong on Imagination
And soon it will be.
Don't rush to frustration
For it's beauty you'll see.

It's a real "Attention Taker"
They say it's the WOW
A "Heavy Bank Maker"
In my Knotting Know How.

As you create a Pretzel
Take your time, read it twice.
You must pay close attention
To create something nice!

If you feel your creations
Have Hemp Master ware.
Just mail us a picture
You can trust we'll be fair.

PROJECTS

Quick Knotting Guide Reference and Abbreviations

Most of the pictured examples for patterns in this section were created with 1.5 mm cord. The knotting was pulled rather tight. The patterns are designed to use different knotting combinations that have proven to be popular in selling to hemp enthusiasts. Don't be afraid to use these patterns as a take off point for experimenting with different knotting styles and combinations. Use imagination and enjoy the outcome of your artistic creation.

The patterns give an estimated length for the jewelry, but knotting combinations may need to be added or subtracted to achieve the length desired. This is especially true if the knotting being done is looser or tighter than the example. The lengths given for the hemp are deliberately on the long side.

To determine the length of knotting to add or subtract, measure a piece of jewelry which is already the desired length and compare it to the length given for the sample piece. Another method is to wrap a piece of hemp around the body part which will be enhanced with the jewelry; compare this length to the length given for the pattern being used and adjust accordingly. Or just measure the piece against the target body part as it is being created. Plan your creation, keeping the center point of the pattern in mind and compare the project to the body part being decorated and the pattern being used.

Wherever possible, add or subtract knots on **both** sides of the middle to maintain the symmetry of the design. The goal, once the center of the pattern is reached, is to reverse the knotting sequence, knot for knot, so that the pattern from the center to either end of the piece is exactly the same. However, if the plan doesn't work as anticipated, don't panic. Just shorten or lengthen the finishing end as needed; in the unlikely event that anyone notices, just tell them it's supposed to be that way! (What a concept!)

Heavy Colored Switch Necklace

Sample Length: 17 inches. This piece can be made in any length and worn as an anklet, bracelet, armband or choker.
Materials: (1) 6 foot length of 1mm colored hemp (dark green in the example) and (1) 6 foot length of 1.5mm natural hemp.

Step 1: Fold the two cords in half and place the colored hemp loop on the outside. Tie a Slide Loop Clasp, starting with the colored hemp as the knotters and the natural hemp as the carriers. After the Switch, the natural cords will become the knotters. Finish the Slide Loop Clasp with 4 Left Square Knots. Don't forget to tie a Half Knot in the colored bead carriers after the second or third of these Square Knots to secure the Slide Loop Clasp.
Step 2: Flip the pattern over or face down.
Step 3: Tie a Switch Knot that is about a half inch long.
Step 4: Tie 4 Left Square Knots. The colored cords will be the knotters for this step.
Step 5: Tie a Switch Knot that is about a half inch long.
Step 6: Tie 4 Left Square Knots. The natural cords will be the knotters for this step.
Step 7: Repeat Steps 2 through 6 until the piece is the desired length (in the example this sequence is repeated 6 times after the SLC).
Step 8: Tie an Overhand Knot in each of the knotters to the side(s) of the last Square Knot. This creates a "T" hook to catch in the Slide Loop Clasp.

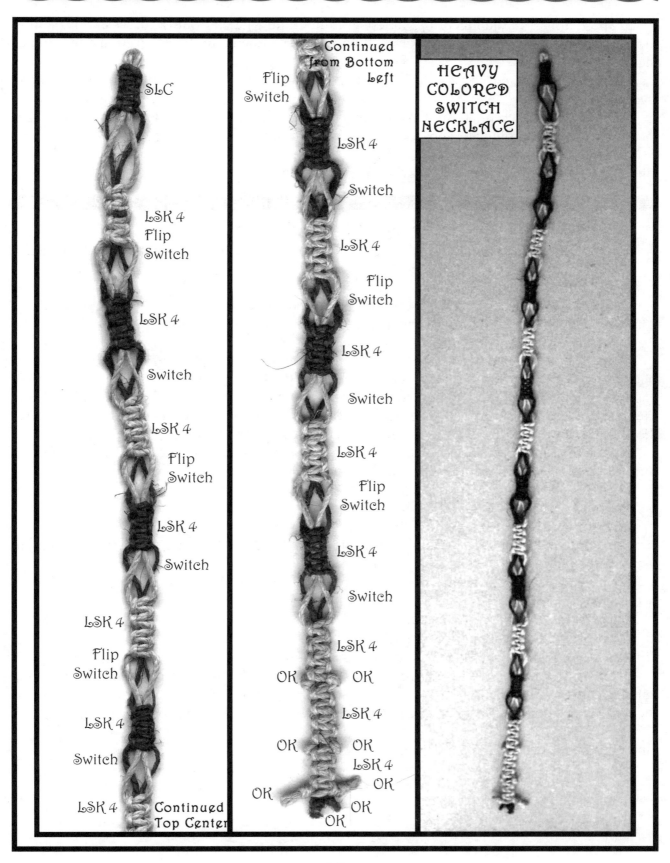

SLC

LSK 4
Flip
Switch

LSK 4

Switch

LSK 4
Flip
Switch

LSK 4

Switch

LSK 4
Flip
Switch

LSK 4

Switch

LSK 4   Continued
Top Center

Continued
from Bottom
Left

Flip
Switch

LSK 4

Switch

LSK 4

Flip
Switch

LSK 4

Switch

LSK 4

Flip
Switch

LSK 4

Switch

LSK 4
OK   OK

LSK 4

OK   OK
LSK 4
OK   OK
OK
OK

HEAVY
COLORED
SWITCH
NECKLACE

35

Step 9: If more adjustment is wanted, continue tying 4 Left Square Knots and repeating Step 8 until satisfied with the number of "T" hooks. The clasp can be secured around any of these "T" hooks.

Step 10: To end, cut the knotters after the last Overhand Knot. Add glue to each of these Overhand Knots.

Step 11: Tie an Overhand Knot in each of the carriers, snug below the last Square Knot. Cut the carriers and add glue to each of these Overhand Knots.

Any ending desired can be used to replace Steps 8 through 11.

PROPER PURPLE CHOKER

This piece can be made in any length and worn as an anklet, bracelet, armband or necklace.

Sample Length: 15 inches
Materials: (1) 6 foot length of 1mm colored hemp (purple in the example), (1) 6 foot length of 1.5mm natural hemp and (29) 4 or 5mm pony/E beads (light purple in the example)

Step 1: Fold the two cords in half and place the colored hemp loop on the outside. Tie a Slide Loop Clasp, starting with the colored hemp as the knotters and the natural hemp as the carriers. After the Switch, the natural cords will become the knotters. Finish the Slide Loop Clasp with 4 Left Square Knots. Don't forget to tie a Half Knot in the colored bead carriers after the second or third of these Square Knots to secure the Slide Loop Clasp.

Step 2: Trade the right colored bead carrier with the right natural knotter. Tie 1 Left Square Knot with the resulting knotters (one colored, one natural).

Step 3: Cut the natural bead carrier so that the next knot will cover the end. Tie 1 Left Square Knot.

Step 4: String the first bead on the colored bead carrier, snug against the last knot tied.

Step 5: Bring the knotters around either side of the bead and tie 2 Left Square Knots snugly beneath the bead.

Step 6: Repeat Steps 4 and 5 until all the beads have been added or until the desired length is reached.

Step 7: Tie 1 more Left Square Knot.

Step 8: Tie an Overhand Knot in each of the knotters to the side(s) of the last Square Knot. This creates a "T" hook to catch in the Slide Loop Clasp.

Step 9: If more adjustment is needed, tie 2 Left Square Knots and repeat Step 8. The clasp can be secured around either "T" hook. To end, tie an Overhand Knot in the carrier, snug below the last Square Knot. Cut off all three cords and add glue to each of the ending Overhand Knots.

Any ending desired can be used to replace Steps 7 through 9.

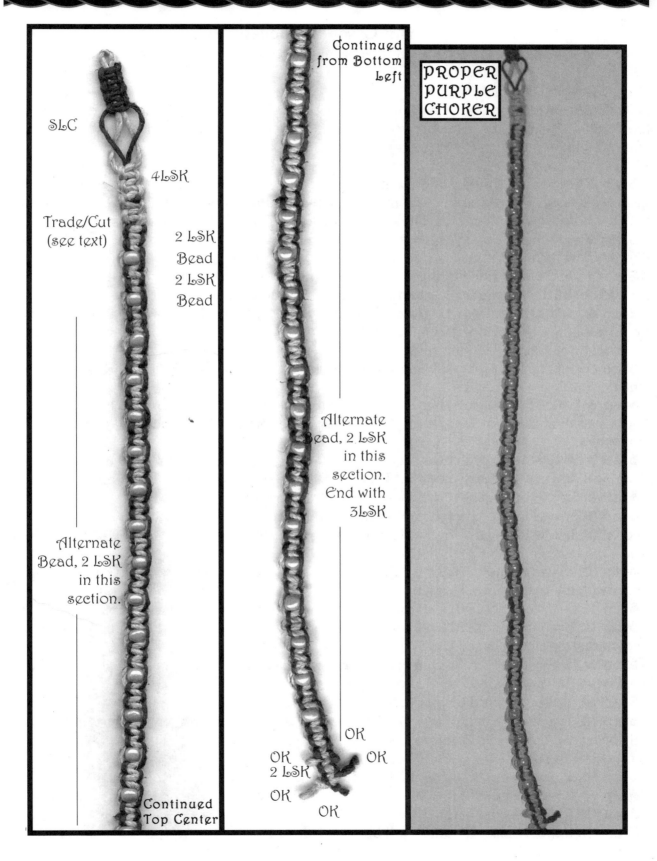

SLC

4LSK

Trade/Cut
(see text)

2 LSK
Bead
2 LSK
Bead

Alternate
Bead, 2 LSK
in this
section.

Continued
Top Center

Continued
from Bottom
Left

Alternate
Bead, 2 LSK
in this
section.
End with
3LSK

OK

OK   OK
2 LSK
OK
        OK

PROPER
PURPLE
CHOKER

Hip Colored Choker
This piece can be wrapped twice around the wrist and worn as a bracelet.

Sample Length: 16.5 inches

Materials: (1) 6 foot length of 1.5mm natural hemp, (1) 6 inch length of 1.5mm natural hemp, (1) 6 foot length of 1mm colored hemp (purple in the example), (5) 9mm crow/pony beads; ((3) crystal and (2) metallic purple in the example).

Step 1: Fold the two natural cords in half and place the short (6") cord loop on the outside. Tie a Slide Loop Clasp, starting with the short cords as the knotters. After the Switch, the long cords will become the knotters. Finish the Slide Loop Clasp with 4 Left Square Knots.

Step 2: Add the 6 foot colored cord, centered across the existing carriers. Tie a Half Knot tight against the added cord (see Page 9).

Step 3: Pinch both sides of the new cord in with the short bead carriers. Tie a second Half Knot to complete the Square Knot and secure the new colored carriers in position.

Step 4: Switch the colored hemp carriers with the natural hemp knotters and tie 4 Left Square Knots (a Square Knot Sinnet) with the new colored knotters. These should be snug against the last Half Knot tied.

Step 5: Cut the short, natural hemp bead carriers so that the ends will be hidden in the next sinnet.

Step 6: Switch the natural hemp carriers with the colored hemp knotters and tie 4 Left Square Knots with the new natural knotters. This Square Knot Sinnet should be snug against the last sinnet tied.

Step 7: Switch the colored hemp carriers with the natural hemp knotters and tie 5 Left Square Knots with the new colored knotters. These should be snug against the last sinnet tied.

Step 8: String the first bead on the carriers (crystal in the example).

Step 9: Bring the knotters (still colored) around either side of the bead and tie a Left Square Knot snug below the bead. Tie another 4 Left Square Knots, giving a total of 5 Square Knots below the bead.

Step 10: Switch the natural hemp carriers with the colored hemp knotters and tie 5 Left Square Knots with the new natural knotters.

Step 11: String the second bead on the carriers (metallic purple in the example).

Step 12: Bring the knotters (still natural) around either side of the bead and tie 5 Left Square Knots snug below the bead.

Step 13: Switch the colored hemp carriers with the natural hemp knotters and tie 3 Left Square Knots with the new colored knotters.

Step 14: String the third (center) bead on the carriers (crystal in the example).

Step 15: The second half of this piece is a mirror image of the first half. To begin tying this half, bring the knotters (still colored) around either side of the bead and tie 3 Left Square Knots snug below the bead.

Step 16: Repeat Steps 10 through 12 (knotters will be natural).

Step 17: Repeat Steps 7 through 9 (knotters will be colored).

Step 18: Repeat Step 6 (knotters will be natural).

Step 19: Repeat Step 4 (knotters will be colored).

Step 20: Switch the natural hemp carriers with the colored hemp knotters and tie 5 Left Square

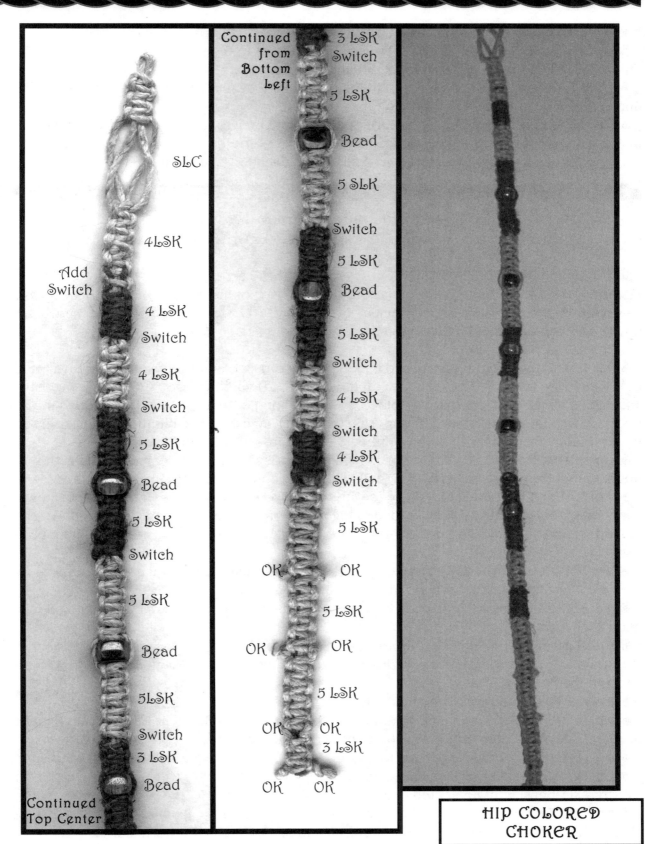

SLC

4LSK

Add Switch

4 LSK
Switch

4 LSK
Switch

5 LSK

Bead

5 LSK

Switch

5 LSK

Bead

5LSK

Switch
3 LSK

Bead

Continued Top Center

Continued from Bottom Left

3 LSK
Switch

5 LSK

Bead

5 SLK

Switch

5 LSK
Bead

5 LSK

Switch

4 LSK

Switch

4 LSK

Switch

5 LSK

OK   OK

5 LSK

OK   OK

5 LSK

OK   OK
            3 LSK

OK   OK

HIP COLORED CHOKER

Knots with the new natural knotters.

Step 21: Tie an Overhand Knot in each of the knotters to the side(s) of the last Square Knot. This creates a "T" hook to catch in the Slide Loop Clasp.

Step 22: Repeat Steps 20 and 21 until the piece is the desired length (switching the knotters and carriers is optional, depending on the desired effect).

Step 23: Before tying the last Square Knot, cut the carriers, add some glue and then tie the last Square Knot over the glue to secure the carriers. Tie an Overhand Knot in each of the knotters and add glue. Any ending desired can be used to replace Steps 21 through 23.

SIMPLE COLORED BRAIDED NECKLACE

This piece can also be wrapped twice around the wrist and worn as a bracelet.

Sample Length: 16 inches
Materials: (1) 3 foot length of 1.5mm natural hemp, (1) 1 foot length of 1.5mm natural hemp, (1) 3 foot length of 1mm colored hemp (black in the example), (1) 1.5 foot length of 1.5mm natural hemp and (1) 3/8 inch diameter metal bead (silver in the example)

Step 1: Fold the 3 foot natural cord 6 inches from one end and fold the 1 foot natural cord in half. Place the loop of the 1 foot cord on the outside. Tie a Slide Loop Clasp, starting with the short cord as the knotters and the folded end of the long cord as the carriers. Finish the Slide Loop Clasp with 4 Left Square Knots. Don't forget to tie a Half Knot in the bead carriers after the second or third of these Square Knots to secure the Slide Loop Clasp.

Step 2: Add the 3 foot colored cord, centered across the existing carriers. Tie a Half Knot tight against the added cord (see Page 9). Leave the ends of the new cord out to the sides.

Step 3: Pinch the natural knotters in with the short bead carriers. Cut the 3 short, natural carriers so that the ends will be hidden in the next series of Square Knots (a sinnet).

Step 4: Use the colored knotters to tie 5 Left Square Knots around all four of the natural carriers.

Step 5: Tie an Overhand Braid using the two colored knotters and the single natural bead carrier. Make this braided section about 5 inches long.

Step 6: Use the colored cords as the knotters and tie 3 Left Square Knots around the single natural carrier.

Step 7: String the center bead on the natural bead carrier snug against the last knot tied. Bring the colored knotters around either side of the bead and tie 3 Left Square Knots snugly beneath the bead.

Step 8: Flip the pattern over or face down.

Step 9: Tie another Overhand Braid using the two colored knotters and the single natural bead carrier. Make this braided section about 5 inches long.

Step 10: Use the colored knotters to tie 3 Left Square Knots around the natural bead carrier.

Step 11: Add the 1.5 foot natural cord, centered across the existing carrier. Tie a Half Knot (colored knotters) tight against the added cord (see Page 9).

Step 12: Pinch both sides of the new natural cord in with the existing bead carrier. Tie a second Half Knot to complete the Square Knot and secure the new natural carriers in position.

Step 13: Cut the old natural carrier so that the end will be hidden in the next Sinnet.

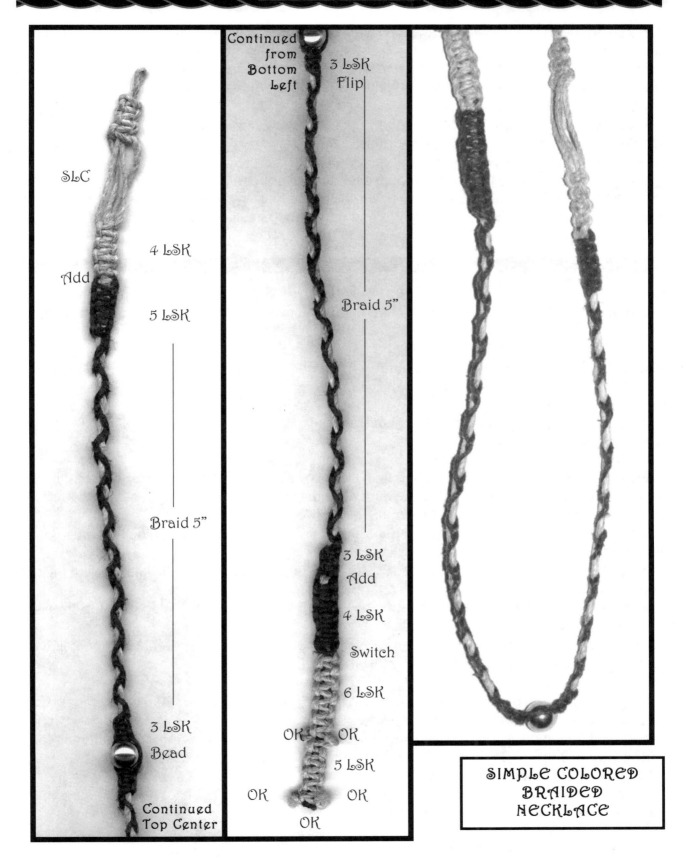

SLC

4 LSK

Add

5 LSK

Braid 5"

3 LSK
Bead

Continued
Top Center

Continued
from
Bottom
Left

3 LSK
Flip

Braid 5"

3 LSK
Add

4 LSK

Switch

6 LSK

OK   OK

5 LSK

OK   OK

OK

SIMPLE COLORED
BRAIDED
NECKLACE

Step 14: Tie another 4 Left Square Knots with the colored knotters (around the 3 natural carriers).

Step 15: Switch the new natural hemp carriers with the colored hemp knotters and tie 4 Left Square Knots with the new natural knotters. This Square Knot Sinnet should be snug against the last sinnet tied.

Step 16: Repeat Steps 14 and 15 until the piece is the desired length. If desired, add a "T" Hook to make the necklace adjustable. (The example ends with 7 natural Square Knots after Step 15 - Hey artists always improvise!)

Step 17: To end, tie an Overhand Knot in each of the knotters, then cut the knotters. Add glue to each of these Overhand Knots. Then tie an Overhand Knot in each of the carriers, snug below the last Square Knot. Cut off the carriers and add glue to each of these Overhand Knots. Any ending desired can be used to replace Steps 15 through 17.

Double Bell Anklet

This piece can be made in any length and worn as a necklace, bracelet, armband or choker.

Sample Length: 11.5 inches
Materials: (2) 4 foot lengths of 1.5mm natural hemp and (8) jingle or sleigh bells with loops (1/4" silver color in the example)

The Ancient Hippies believe that the sounds of bells together will ward off evil spirits. So get your bells on! And Be Hempy!

Step 1: Fold the two cords in half and tie a Slide Loop Clasp. Finish with 6 Left Square Knots. Don't forget to tie a Half Knot in the carriers after the second or third of these Square Knots to prevent the carriers from slipping when the clasp is opened.

Step 2: Pick one side of the Square Knot Sinnet for the bells and place a bell on the knotter, which is on that side.

Step 3: Tie 1 Alternating Half Knot, being sure to leave a small loop in the knotter with the bell so that the bell can move freely.

Step 4: Tie 2 Alternating Half Knots (start each Half Knot on the opposite side from the previous one tied).

Step 5: Place a second bell on the chosen side and tie 1 Alternating Half Knot, again leaving a small loop in the knotter so that the bell will move freely.

Step 6: Tie 14 Alternating Half Knots.

Step 7: Repeat Steps 2 through 6 four more times (for a total of 5 knotting sequences). Continue repeating if a longer project is desired.

Step 8: Flip the piece over (face down) and tie a Switch Knot, which is about a half inch long. Secure the switch with 2 Alternating Half Knots.

Step 9: Repeat Step 8 three more times.

Step 10: To end, tie 1 Overhand Knot in each cord, snug to the last knot tied. Cut each of the cords and add glue to each of these knots.

Any ending desired can be used to replace Step 10.

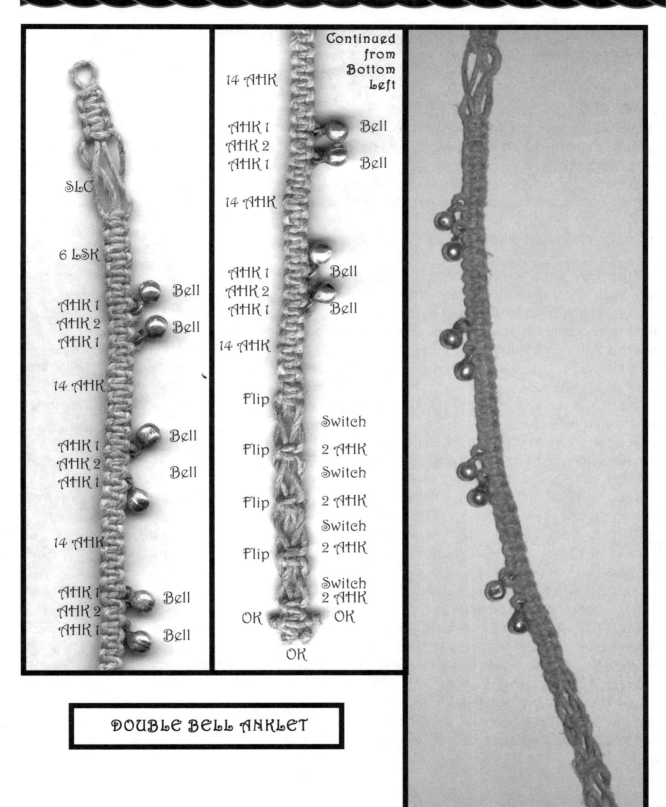

SLC

6 LSK

AHK 1
AHK 2   Bell
AHK 1   Bell

14 AHK

AHK 1   Bell
AHK 2   Bell
AHK 1

14 AHK

AHK 1   Bell
AHK 2   Bell
AHK 1

Continued
from
Bottom
Left

14 AHK

AHK 1   Bell
AHK 2
AHK 1   Bell

14 AHK

AHK 1   Bell
AHK 2
AHK 1   Bell

14 AHK

Flip

Flip   Switch
              2 AHK
Flip   Switch
              2 AHK
Flip   Switch
              2 AHK
              Switch
              2 AHK
OK   OK
       OK

DOUBLE BELL ANKLET

43

Loopy Colored Bell Anklet

Length (and bells) can be added to this piece on either side of the twisted sinnets and it can be worn as a necklace or choker.

Sample Length: 11.75 inches

Materials: (1) 4 foot length of 1mm colored hemp (black in the example), (1) 4 foot length of 1mm colored hemp (purple in the example) and (12) jingle or sleigh bells with loops (1/4" silver color in the example)

The Ancient Hippies believe that the sounds of bells together will ward off evil spirits.

So get your bells on! And Be Hempy!

Step 1: Fold the two cords in half. Begin with the black cord on the outside as the knotters. Tie a Slide Loop Clasp, finishing with 7 Left Square Knots (knotters should be purple after the switch). Don't forget to tie a Half Knot in the carriers after the second or third of these Square Knots to prevent the carriers from slipping when the clasp is opened.

Step 2: Place 3 bells on the carriers (black) and create a half inch loop in these carriers so the bells will hang and swing freely. Tie 7 Left Square Knots (purple knotters) snug to the last knot tied.

Step 3: Switch the carriers with the knotters and tie 21 Left Half Knots (a left twist sinnet) with the new black knotters.

Step 4: Place 3 bells on the carriers (purple) and create a half inch loop in these carriers so the bells will hang and swing freely. Tie 21 Right Half Knots (a right twist sinnet) snug to the last knot tied.

Step 5: Switch the carriers with the knotters and tie 7 Left Square Knots with the new purple knotters. These should be snug to the last knot tied.

Step 6: Place 3 bells on the carriers (black) and create a half inch loop in these carriers so the bells will hang and swing freely. Tie 7 Left Square Knots (purple knotters) snug to the last knot tied.

Step 7: Switch the carriers with the knotters and tie 7 Left Square Knots with the new black knotters. These should be snug to the last knot tied.

Step 8: Repeat Step 7 switching colors until the piece is the length desired. More bells and loops may be added along the way, if desired. Also, Overhand Knots may be tied in the knotters (before switching) to create T-hooks for securing the Slide Loop Clasp.

Step 9: Finish with three bells on the carriers; loop the carriers back on themselves and cut the ends before tying the last knots. Then tie the last Square Knots over the doubled carriers to hide and secure the cut ends. Tie 1 Overhand Knot in each of the knotters and cut the remaining cord snug to the overhand knot. Add glue to each of these knots.

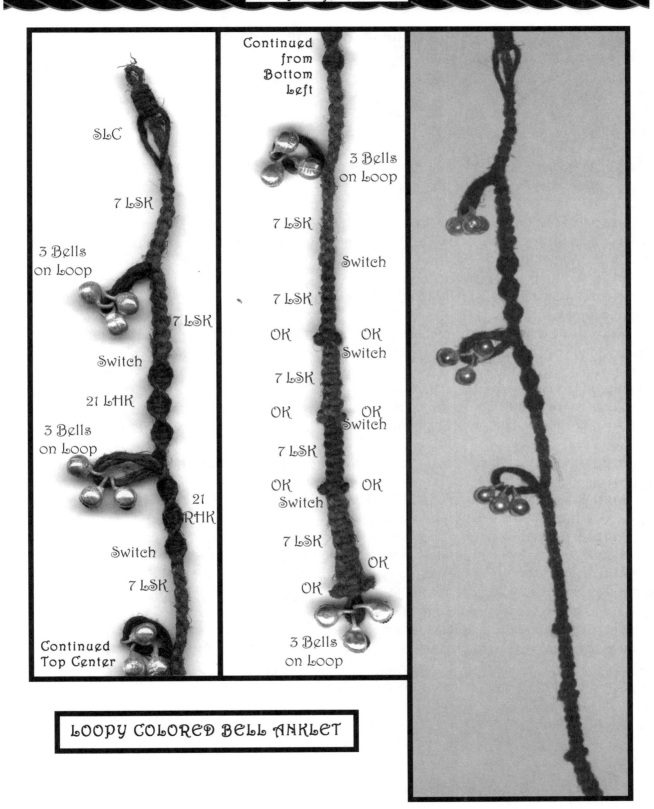

SLC

7 LSK

3 Bells
on Loop

7 LSK

Switch

21 LHK

3 Bells
on Loop

21
RHK

Switch

7 LSK

Continued
Top Center

Continued
from
Bottom
Left

3 Bells
on Loop

7 LSK

Switch

7 LSK

OK

7 LSK

OK

7 LSK

OK
Switch

7 LSK

OK

OK
Switch

OK
Switch

OK

OK

7 LSK

OK

3 Bells
on Loop

LOOPY COLORED BELL ANKLET

Double Bell Necklace

This piece can be made in any length and worn as an anklet, bracelet, armband or choker.

Sample Length: 18 inches
Materials: (2) 6 foot lengths of 1.5mm natural hemp and (16) jingle or sleigh bells with loops (1/4" silver color in the example)

The Ancient Hippies believe that the sounds of bells together will ward off evil spirits.
So get your bells on! And Be Hempy!

Step 1: Fold the two cords in half and tie a Slide Loop Clasp. Finish with 7 Left Square Knots. Don't forget to tie a Half Knot in the carriers after the second or third of these Square Knots to prevent the carriers from slipping when the clasp is opened.

Step 2: Flip the piece over (face down).

Step 3: Place a bell on the right bead carrier and a second bell on the right knotter, snug to the last knot tied.

Step 4: Tie a Switch Knot that is about a half inch long. Position the bells so that the bell on the original knotter hangs from the first (top) loop of the Switch Knot and the bell on the original carrier hangs from the second (bottom) loop of the Switch Knot (see project photo). All bells remain on the same side of the necklace.

Step 5: Tie 7 Left Square Knots, using the new set of knotters.

Step 6: Place a bell on the right bead carrier and a second bell on the right knotter, snug to the last knot tied.

Step 7: Flip the piece over (face down) so that all the bells are now on the left side of the piece.

Step 8: Repeat Steps 4 through 7 until the necklace is 2 to 4 inches less than the total length desired (6 times in the example).

Step 9: Repeat Steps 3, 4 and 5 one more time to tie in the last set of bells.

Step 10: Tie a Switch Knot that is about a half inch long.

Step 11: If the project is already long enough, skip to Step 12 to end the project. To continue the pattern, tie 7 Left Square Knots, followed by a half inch Switch Knot. Repeat this step as needed to reach the desired length.

Step 12: To end, tie 4 Left Square Knots. Tie an Overhand Knot in each of the 4 cords, cut each of the cords and add glue to each of the ending Overhand Knots

Any ending desired can be used to replace Steps 11 and 12.

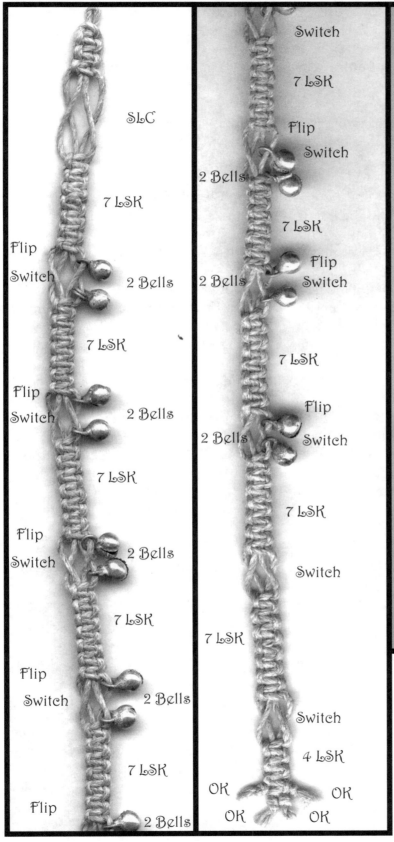

SLC

7 LSK

Flip
Switch

2 Bells

7 LSK

Flip
Switch

2 Bells

7 LSK

Flip
Switch

2 Bells

7 LSK

Flip
Switch

2 Bells

7 LSK

Flip

2 Bells

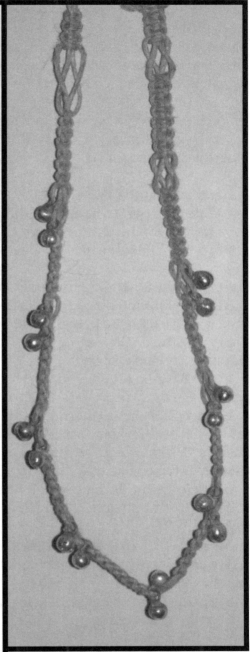

Switch

7 LSK

Flip
Switch

2 Bells

7 LSK

Flip
Switch

2 Bells

7 LSK

Flip
Switch

2 Bells

7 LSK

Switch

7 LSK

Switch

4 LSK

OK   OK
   OK   OK

DOUBLE
BELL NECKLACE

47

Good Fortune Belly Chain

Sample Length: 35 inches
Materials: (2) 10 foot lengths of 1.5mm natural hemp and (24) jingle or sleigh bells with loops (1/4" silver color in the example)

The Ancient Hippies believe that the sounds of bells together will ward off evil spirits. So get your bells on! And Be Hempy! This piece makes a great sound walking around and it is even better for a belly dancer!

Step 1: Fold the two cords in half and tie a Slide Loop Clasp. Finish with 4 Left Square Knots. Don't forget to tie a Half Knot in the carriers after the second or third of these Square Knots to prevent the carriers from slipping when the clasp is opened.

Step 2: Flip the piece over (face down) and tie a Switch Knot that is about 3/4 of an inch long.

Step 3: Tie 3 Left Square Knots, using the new set of knotters.

Step 4: Flip the piece over (face down) and tie a Switch Knot that is about 3/4 of an inch long.

Step 5: Tie 5 Alternating Half Knots (to do this, start each Half Knot on the opposite side from the previous one tied).

Step 6: Choose a side of the project for the bells to hang from and place a bell on that knotter.

Step 7: Tie 1 more Alternating Half Knot. Leave a small loop in the knotter with the bell so that the bell will be able to move freely (see photo of project).

Step 8: Repeat Steps 6 and 7 twice, so that there are a total of three bells in this section. Be sure that all the bells are on the same side of this Half Knot sinnet.

Step 9: Tie 5 Alternating Half Knots.

Step 10: Flip the piece over (face down) and tie a Switch Knot that is about 3/4 of an inch long.

Step 11: Tie 3 Left Square Knots.

Step 12: Repeat Steps 2 through 11 until the belly chain is the desired length (6 times in the example).

Step 13: When all but the last three bells have been added and the knotting sequence in Step 12 is completed, more length may still be desired. If so, switch to repeating Steps 10 and 11 (3 times in the example).

Step 14: Before tying the last sinnet, cut one of the carriers so that the end will be hidden in this last series of knots.

Step 15: To end, tie an Overhand Knot using all three of the remaining cords. Tie a second Overhand Knot in the three cords, one inch from the first knot. These Overhand Knots can be used to catch the Slide Loop Clasp when wearing the belly chain.

Step 16: Place a bell on each remaining cord. About 1 1/2" from the second overhand knot, make a small loop in each cord, place the bell in the loop and tie two Half Hitches around the cord to secure the loop. Cut the extra cord and save it for future filler. Add glue to each of the double Half Hitches.

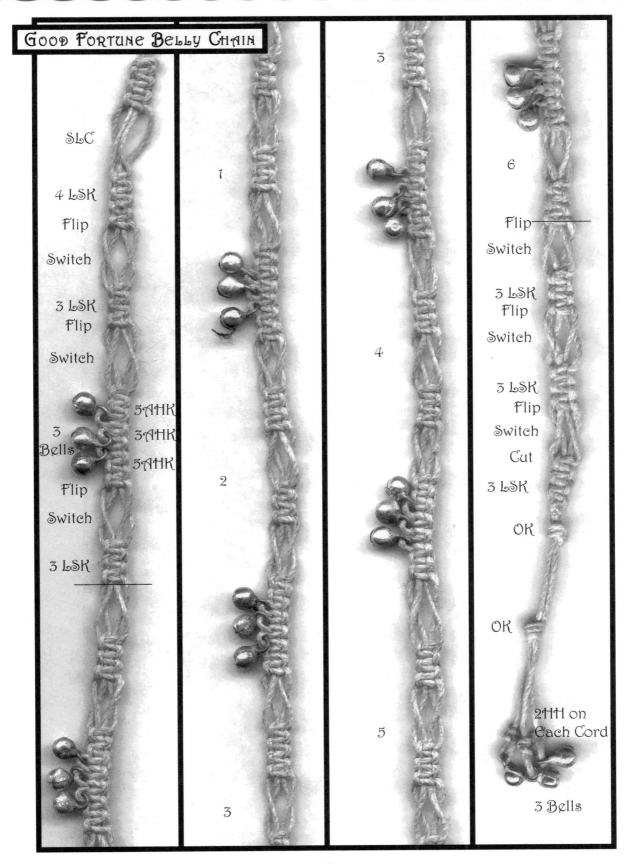

GOOD FORTUNE BELLY CHAIN

SLC

4 LSK
Flip

Switch

3 LSK
Flip

Switch

3
Bells   5AHK
         3AHK
Flip   5AHK
Switch

3 LSK

1

2

3

3

4

5

6

Flip
Switch

3 LSK
Flip
Switch

3 LSK
Flip
Switch
Cut
3 LSK

OK

OK

2HH on
Each Cord

3 Bells

GOOD FORTUNE BELLY CHAIN

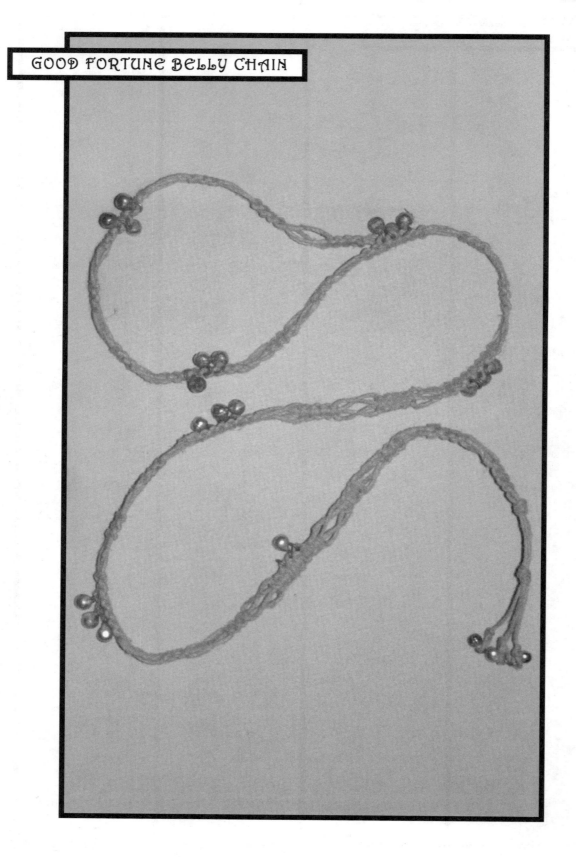

SPENCERVILLE PUBLIC LIBRARY
498 E. PLEASANT ST.
SPENCERVILLE, OH 45804

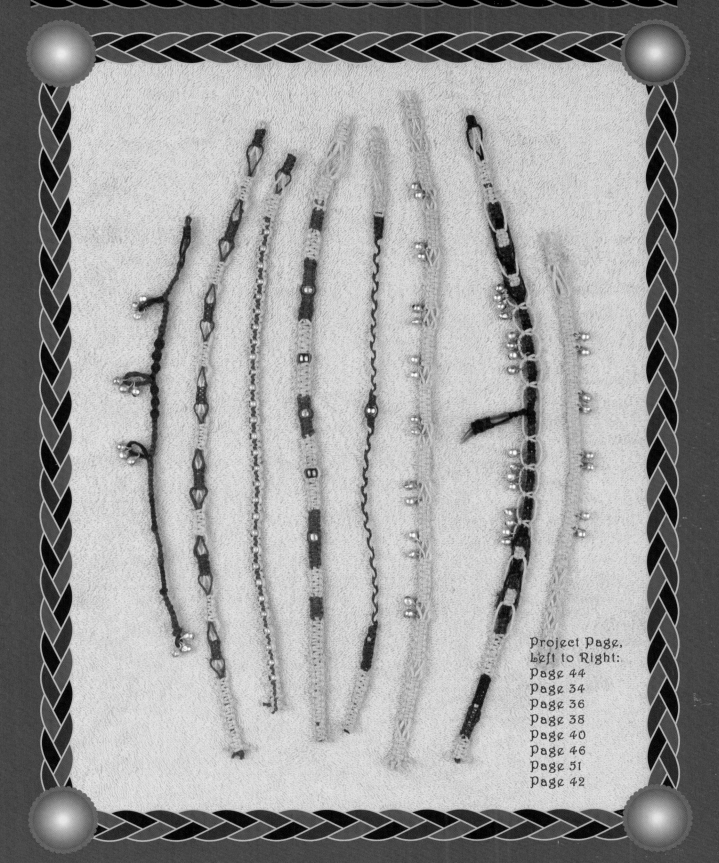

Project Page,
Left to Right:
Page 44
Page 34
Page 36
Page 38
Page 40
Page 46
Page 51
Page 42

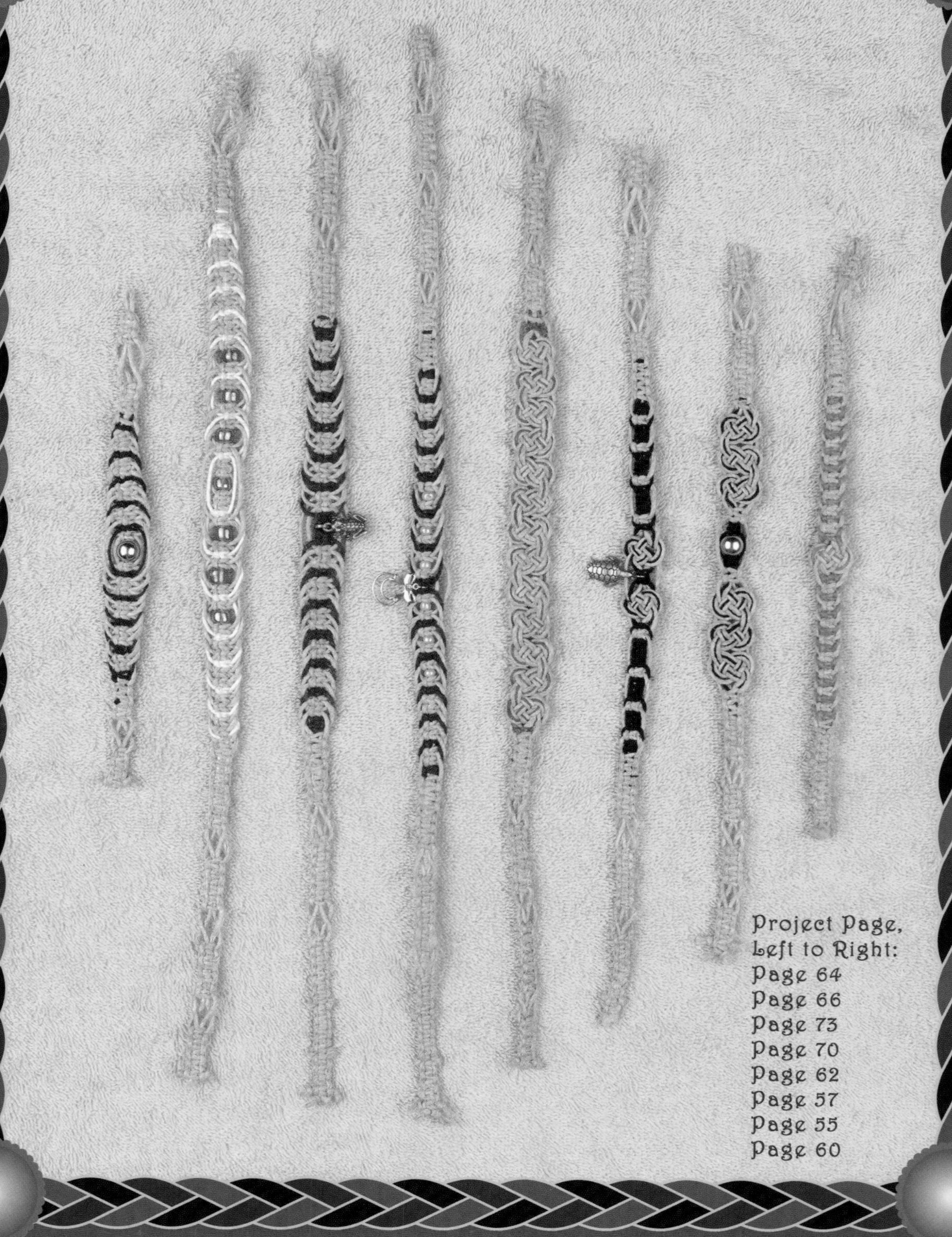

Project Page,
Left to Right:
Page 64
Page 66
Page 73
Page 70
Page 62
Page 57
Page 55
Page 60

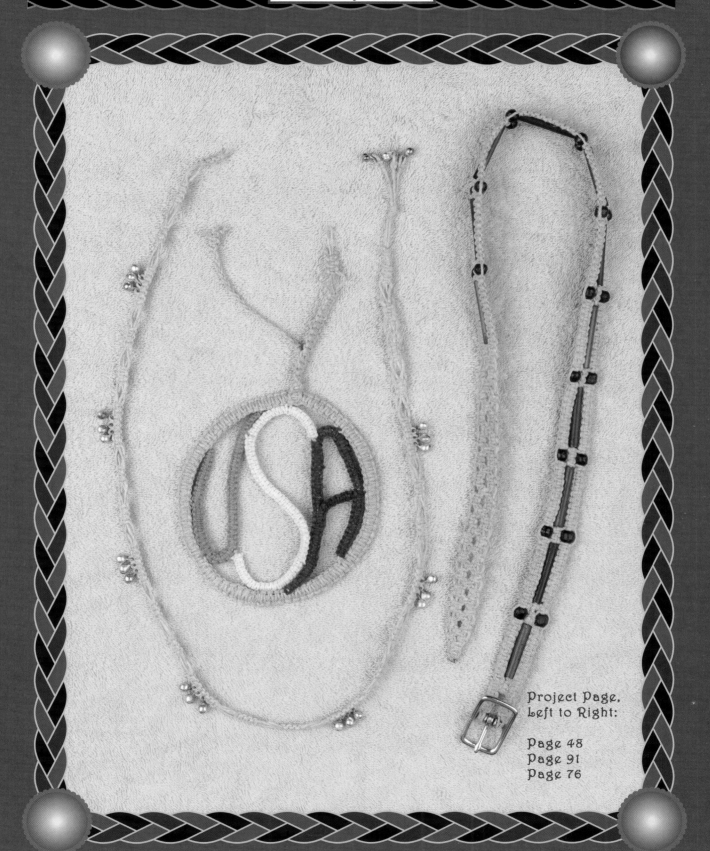

Project Page,
Left to Right:

Page 48
Page 91
Page 76

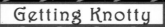

Project Page,
Top to Bottom

Page 80
Page 87
Page 84

Looped Jade and Bells Necklace

Sample Length: 17 1/4 inches

Materials: (1) 4 foot length of 1.5mm natural hemp, (1) 4 foot length of 1mm colored hemp (purple in the example), (1) 4 foot length of 1mm colored hemp (black in the example), (1) 2 foot length of 0.5mm natural hemp, (1) 6 inch length of 1mm colored hemp (black in the example) , (16) jingle or sleigh bells with loops (1/4" silver color in the example) and (1) jade charm (jade tusk in the example)

The charm for this piece should be larger on one end (e.g. tapered) so that it can be securely tied into the knotting. If it is not tapered, it may be necessary to cut a groove or hole in the charm so that it will hold a wrap and will not fall out of the knotted sinnet. This piece can be wrapped twice around the wrist and worn as a bracelet. The Ancient Hippies believe that the sounds of bells together will ward off evil spirits. So get your bells on! And Be Hempy!

Step 1: Fold the natural and black cords in half. Begin with the black cord on the outside as the knotters. Begin to tie a Slide Loop Clasp (knotters should be natural after the switch). Tie 3 or 4 Left Square Knots after the Switch Knot.

Step 2: Add the 2 foot length of thin natural hemp as a third carrier (in the center of the other two carriers; see page 8). At the same time, add the 4 foot purple cord, centered across the existing carriers. Tie a Half Knot tight against the added cords (see Page 9). Pinch both sides of the purple cord in with the three other carriers. Tie a second Half Knot to complete the Left Square Knot and secure the new carriers in position. There are now 5 carriers: 2 black, 2 purple and one thin natural carrier. Continue tying Left Square Knots until a total of 7 have been tied after the Switch Knot. This completes the Slide Loop Clasp.

Step 3: Leave the natural knotters out to the side. Use the purple hemp cords as knotters and tie 3 Left Square Knots over the 3 remaining carriers (2 black and 1 thin natural). There are now two sets of knotters and a set of 3 carriers.

Step 4: Put the purple knotters to either side. Use the black carriers as knotters and tie 3 Left Square Knots around the single remaining thin bead carrier. There are now three sets of knotters (a natural set, the purple set, and the black set) and a single thin bead carrier.

Step 5: Bring the natural knotters over (in front of) the purple and black knotters, leaving them looped around the purple and black knots just tied. Tie 3 Left Square Knots around the single thin carrier (just below the last black knot tied).

Step 6: Bring the purple knotters over (in front of) the black and natural knotters, leaving them looped around the black and natural knots just tied. Tie 3 Left Square Knots around the single thin carrier (just below the last natural knot tied).

Step 7: Bring the black knotters over (in front of) the natural and purple knotters, leaving them looped around the natural and purple knots just tied. Tie 3 Left Square Knots around the single thin carrier (just below the last purple knot tied).

Step 8: Repeat Step 5, but only tie 2 Left Square Knots with the natural knotters.

Step 9: Repeat Step 6, but only tie 2 Left Square Knots with the purple knotters. Gather the purple knotters in with the single carrier.

Step 10: Bring the black knotters over (in front of) the natural knotters and tie 2 Left Square Knots around all three carriers (purple and thin natural). Gather the black knotters in with the

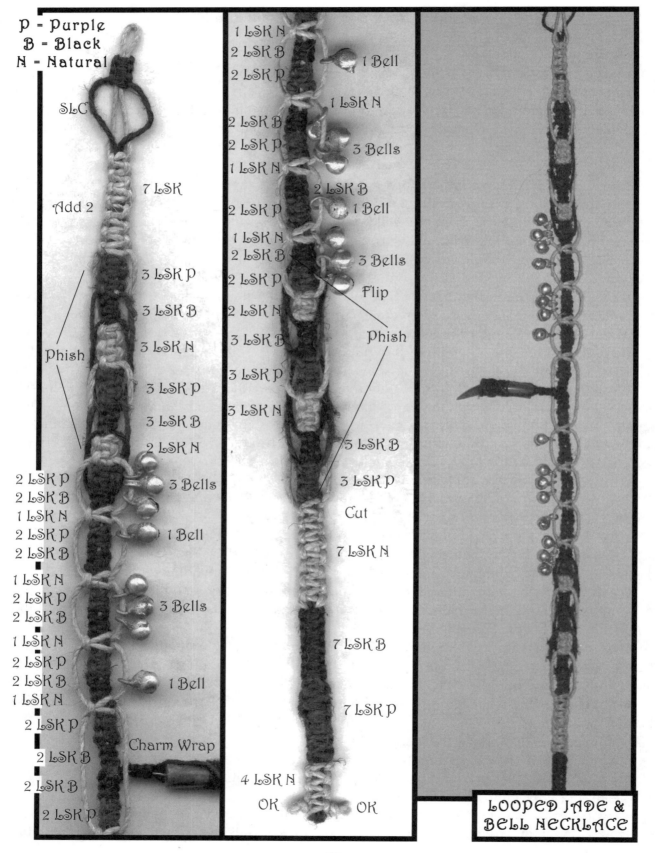

P = Purple
B = Black
N = Natural

SLC

7 LSK

Add 2

Phish

3 LSK P

3 LSK B

3 LSK N

3 LSK P

3 LSK B

2 LSK N

2 LSK P
2 LSK B
1 LSK N
2 LSK P
2 LSK B

1 LSK N
2 LSK P
2 LSK B

1 LSK N
2 LSK P
2 LSK B
1 LSK N

2 LSK P

2 LSK B

2 LSK B

2 LSK P

3 Bells

1 Bell

3 Bells

1 Bell

Charm Wrap

1 LSK N
2 LSK B
2 LSK P

2 LSK B
2 LSK P
1 LSK N

2 LSK B
2 LSK P

2 LSK B

1 LSK N
2 LSK B
2 LSK P

2 LSK N

3 LSK B

3 LSK P

3 LSK N

1 Bell

1 LSK N

3 Bells

1 Bell

3 Bells

Flip

Phish

3 LSK B

3 LSK P

Cut

7 LSK N

7 LSK B

7 LSK P

4 LSK N

OK   OK

LOOPED JADE &
BELL NECKLACE

other carriers.

Step 11: Use the natural knotters and place 3 bells on one of the knotter (choose a side). Loop the knotters around the purple and black knots just tied. Leave enough slack in the loops for the bells to hang freely and tie 1 Left Square Knot around all five carriers (black, purple and thin natural). Leave the natural knotters out to the side.

Step 12: Use the purple cords as knotters and tie 2 Left Square Knots around the three remaining carriers (2 black and 1 thin natural). Gather the purple cords back in with the carriers.

Step 13: Use the black cords as knotters and tie 2 Left Square Knots around the three remaining carriers (2 purple and 1 thin natural). Gather the black cords back in with the carriers.

Step 14: Use the natural knotters and place 1 bell on the correct knotter. Loop the knotters around the purple and black knots just tied. Make the loops the same size as in Step 11 and tie 1 Left Square Knot around all five carriers (2 black, 2 purple and 1 thin natural). Leave the natural knotters out to the side.

Step 15: Repeat Steps 12 and 13.

Step 16: Repeat Step 11.

Step 17: Repeat Step 14.

Step 18: Repeat Steps 12 and 13.

Step 19: Use the 6-inch length of black cord to tie a hemp wrap around the charm. Exactly how the charm is secured depends on the charm used. The key is to make sure the charm hangs below the main knot work. In the example, the author used a tapered jade tusk about an inch and a half long with a small copper wire sticking out of the top (originally a small wire loop, which was straightened). It is not necessary to have a wire, but it does make the charm easier to secure in the wrap. Think of the charm as a bead carrier and tie the knotters around it. Place the center of the cord about two-thirds of the way down the charm (on the small end) and tie a tight Left Square Knot around the charm. Tie 9 more Left Square Knots around the charm (this LSK Sinnet creates the spiral effect seen on the tusk). Slide the sinnet towards the larger end (top) of the charm to make the wrap as tight and secure as possible. Bring the ends of the cord up opposite sides of the charm and tie 2 Left Square Knots around the wire at the top, as close to the charm as possible. Follow this with 2 Right Square Knots, then 3 Alternating Square Knots. Gather the ends of the charm knotters in with the three carriers in the main piece. Cut them short so the ends will be hidden in the next series of knots. The remainder of the piece is a mirror image of the first half, plus whatever extra length is needed. Simply work backwards if you have it all figured out. If not, follow the remaining steps.

Step 20: Repeat Step 13 (black knotters), tying the knots around the three carriers plus the cords used to attach the charm, then repeat Step 12 with the purple knotters.

Step 22: Use the natural knotters and loop them around all the knots just tied (go behind the charm). Tie 1 Left Square Knot around all five carriers. Leave the natural knotters out to the side.

Step 23: Repeat Steps 13 and 12 (black knotters followed by purple knotters).

Step 24: Repeat Step 14 (1 bell, on the natural knotters).

Step 25: Repeat Steps 13 and 12 (black knotters followed by purple knotters).

Step 26: Repeat Step 11 (3 bells on the natural knotters).

Step 27: Repeat Steps 13 and 12 (black knotters followed by purple knotters).

Step 28: Repeat Step 14 (1 bell, on the natural knotters).

Step 29: Repeat Step 13 (black knotters), but leave the black knotters out to the side.

Step 30: Use the purple cords as knotters and tie 2 Left Square Knots around the remaining thin natural carrier. Leave the purple knotters out to the side.

Step 31: Flip over the project. (Not you, flip the project face down.) This step is needed to make the second half of the Phish Bone pattern match the first half (a mirror image out to each end).

Step 32: Bring the natural knotters over (in front of) the purple and black knotters, leaving them looped around the purple and black knots just tied. Place 3 bells on the correct knotter and tie 2 Left Square Knots around the single thin carrier (just below the last purple knot tied).

Step 33: Repeat Step 7, leaving the black knotters out to the side.

Step 34: Repeat Step 6, leaving the purple knotters out to the side.

Step 35: Repeat Step 5, leaving the natural knotters out to the side.

Step 36: Repeat Step 7, but gather the black knotters in with the thin natural carrier.

Step 37: Repeat Step 6, but gather the purple knotters in with the three other carriers.

Step 38: Bring the natural knotters over (in front of) the purple and black knotters, leaving them looped around the purple and black knots just tied. Tie 1 Left Square Knot around the five carriers. Cut the thin natural carrier so that the end will be hidden in the remainder of this Square Knot sinnet. This sinnet will complete the mirror image of the first half of the pattern. If no more length is needed, cut the ends of the black and purple cords as well. Tie 6 more Left Square Knots.

Step 39: To add more length, gather the natural knotters in as carriers and bring the black cords out as knotters. Tie 7 Left Square Knots around the natural and purple carriers. Gather the black cords in as carriers and bring the purple cords out as knotters. Tie 7 Left Square Knots around the natural and black carriers. Continue tying Left Square Knot sinnets, alternating natural, black and purple knotters until the desired length is reached.

Step 40: To end, cut the carriers, put glue on the cut ends and tie 1 last Square Knot over the glued ends. Tie an Overhand Knot in each of the knotters. Cut the cords and add glue to each of these Overhand Knots.

Center Bead Pretzel Anklet

This piece can be adjusted in length before and after the Pretzel Knot section and worn as a bracelet, armband or choker.

Sample Length: 11 3/4 inches

Materials: (2) 5 foot lengths of 1.5mm natural hemp, (1) 3 foot length of 1mm colored hemp (black in the example), (1) 3/8 inch diameter metal bead (silver in the example)

Step 1: Fold the two natural hemp cords in half and tie a Slide Loop Clasp. Finish with 7 Left Square Knots.

Step 2: Add the 3 foot colored cord, centered across the existing carriers. Tie a Half Knot tight against the added cord (see Page 9).

Step 3: Pinch both sides of the new cord in with the existing bead carriers. Tie a second Half Knot to complete the Square Knot and secure the new colored carriers in position.

Step 4: Split the 6 cords into two sets of three cords. The colored cord should be in the middle of each set and the natural knotter to the outside.

Step 5: Leave a space of about 1/8 inch in the cords and then tie a slightly loose Pretzel Knot with the two sets of cords. (The knot in the example is approximately 3/4 of an inch wide and 1/2 inch long.) Keep the cords parallel, with the colored one in the middle, in all portions of the knot to maintain the colored design.

Step 6: Tie two more Pretzel Knots that are the same size as the first. Be sure to start each Pretzel Knot on the opposite side from the previous knot tied to prevent the pattern from twisting. Adjust these knots so that they just barely touch one another and are not too tight. The small spaces between the cords and knots are part of the design.

Step 7: Gather the cords back into the previous set (2 natural knotters and 4 carriers, 2 colored and 2 natural).

Step 8: Tie 3 Alternating Half Knots (i.e. left, right, and left) around the 4 carriers.

Step 9: Leave the natural knotters out to the side and use the colored cords to tie 2 Left Square Knots around the remaining 2 natural carriers.

Step 10: With the natural knotters still out to the side, string the bead on the natural carriers, snug against the last knot tied.

Step 11: Bring the colored knotters around either side of the bead and tie 2 Left Square Knots snugly beneath the bead. Pull the colored cords back in as carriers.

Step 12: Bring the natural knotters around either side of the bead and the knots just tied and use them to tie 2 Left Square Knots around the 4 carriers (2 natural, 2 colored).

Step 13: Repeat Steps 4 through 6.

Step 14: Pinch the colored knotters in with the natural carriers and use the natural knotters to tie 1 Left Square Knot over these 4 carriers.

Step 15: Cut the colored carriers so that the ends will be hidden in the following series of knots.

Step 16: Tie 6 Left Square Knots around the natural carriers and the cut colored carriers.

Step 17: Tie a Switch Knot, which is about 3/8 inch long.

Step 18: Tie 4 Left Square Knots.

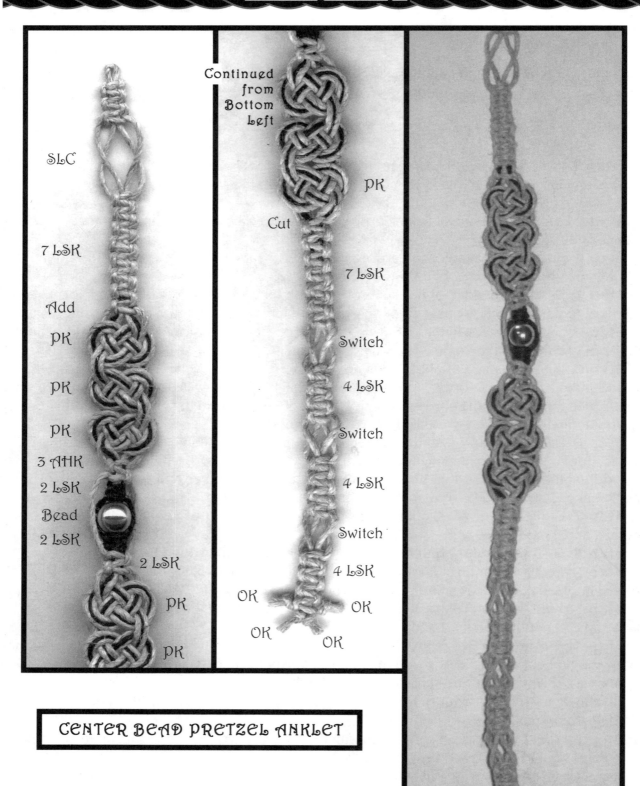

SLC

7 LSK

Add
PK

PK

PK

3 AHK
2 LSK
Bead
2 LSK

2 LSK
PK

PK

Continued
from
Bottom
Left

PK

Cut

7 LSK

Switch

4 LSK

Switch

4 LSK

Switch

4 LSK

OK   OK

OK   OK

CENTER BEAD PRETZEL ANKLET

Step 19: Repeat Steps 17 and 18 until the piece is the desired length. To end, tie an Overhand Knot in each of the cords. Cut off the cords and add glue to each of these Overhand Knots. Any ending desired can be used to replace this step.

Turtle Love Pretzel Necklace

This piece can be shortened in length before and after the Pretzel Knot section and worn as a bracelet, armband or choker.

Sample Length: 15 inches

Materials: (2) 7 foot lengths of 1.5mm natural hemp, (1) 3 foot length of 1mm colored hemp (black in the example) and (1) 3/4 inch turtle charm (pewter with a loop in the example)

Step 1: Fold the two natural cords in half and tie a Slide Loop Clasp. Finish with 7 Square Knots.

Step 2: Tie a Switch Knot, which is about 1/2 inch long.

Step 3: Tie 3 Square Knots.

Step 4: Add the 3 foot colored cord, centered across the existing carriers. Tie a Half Knot tight against the added cord (see Page 9).

Step 5: Pinch both sides of the new cord in with the existing bead carriers. Tie a second Half Knot to complete the Square Knot and secure the new colored carriers in position.

Step 6: Tie 3 more Square Knots. Leave the natural knotters out to the side.

Step 7: Use the colored cords as knotters and tie 2 Square Knots around the remaining 2 natural carriers. Leave the new colored knotters out to the side (through Step 14 leave the knotters just used out to the side).

Step 8: Bring the natural knotters over the colored knotters and tie 1 Square Knot.

Step 9: Bring the colored knotters over the natural knotters and tie 3 Square Knots.

Step 10: Bring the natural knotters over the colored knotters and tie 1 Square Knot.

Step 11: Bring the colored knotters over the natural knotters and tie 4 Square Knots.

Step 12: Bring the natural knotters over the colored knotters and tie 1 Square Knot.

Step 13: Bring the colored knotters over the natural knotters and tie 5 Square Knots.

Step 14: Bring the natural knotters over the colored knotters and tie 1 Square Knot.

Step 15: Bring the colored knotters over the natural knotters and tie 1 Square Knot.

Step 16: Split the 6 cords into two sets of three cords. The colored cord should be in the middle of each set and the natural knotter to the outside.

Step 17: Tie a Pretzel Knot with the two sets of cords. (The knot in the example is between 1/2 and 3/4 of an inch wide and 1/2 inch long.) Keep the cords parallel, with the colored one in the middle, in all portions of the knot to maintain the colored design. Leave the natural knotters out to the side.

Step 18: Use the colored knotters and tie 1 Left Half Knot around the natural carriers.

Step 19: String the carriers and the left colored knotter through the loop on the charm. Bring the other colored knotter around the charm loop and tie 1 Right Half Knot snugly beneath the charm. (In the example a jump ring was attached to the charm and the cords strung through the jump ring so that the charm would hang properly. Other adjustments may be necessary depending on the type of charm used.)

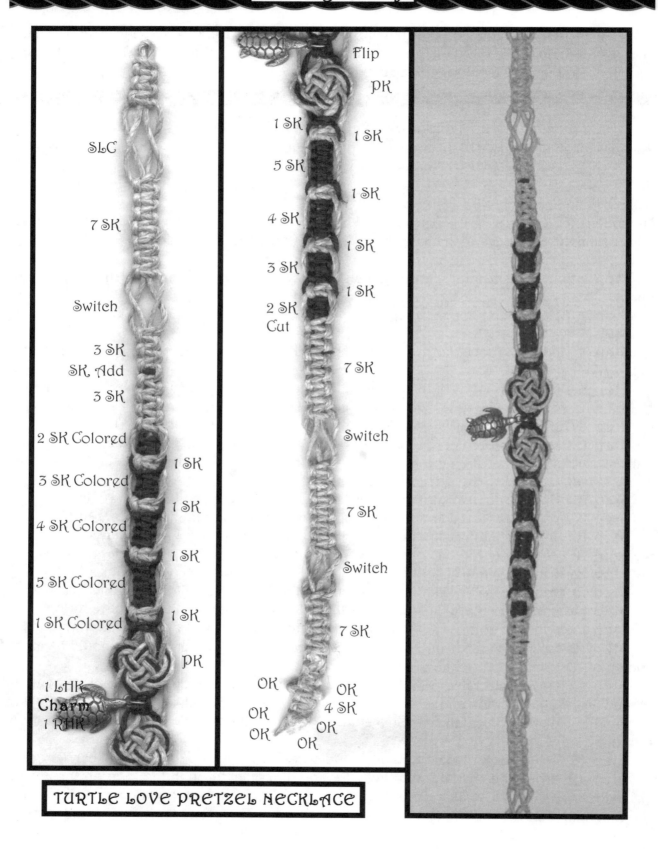

SLC

7 SK

Switch

3 SK
SK, Add
3 SK

2 SK Colored

3 SK Colored   1 SK

4 SK Colored   1 SK

5 SK Colored   1 SK

1 SK Colored   1 SK

                                PK

1 LHK
Charm
1 RHK

Flip
                                PK

1 SK   1 SK

5 SK   1 SK

4 SK   1 SK

3 SK   1 SK

2 SK
Cut

                        7 SK

                        Switch

                        7 SK

                        Switch

                        7 SK

OK   OK

OK   4 SK

OK   OK

                OK

TURTLE LOVE PRETZEL NECKLACE

58

Step 20: Flip the pattern over (or face down), so that the back of the charm faces up. The second half of the pattern is a mirror image of the first half and is tied with the necklace in this position.

Step 21: Bring the natural knotters down to the rest of the cords; the right knotter will pass over the back of the charm. Split the 6 cords into two sets of three cords with the colored cord in the middle of each set and the natural knotter to the outside.

Step 22: Tie a Pretzel Knot to match the first Pretzel Knot tied. Remember to keep the cords parallel, with the colored one in the middle, in all portions of the knot. Leave the natural knotters out to the side.

Step 23: Use the colored knotters to tie 1 Square Knot around the natural carriers.

Step 24: Bring the natural knotters over the colored knotters and tie 1 Square Knot.

Step 25: Bring the colored knotters over the natural knotters and tie 5 Square Knots.

Step 26: Bring the natural knotters over the colored knotters and tie 1 Square Knot.

Step 27: Bring the colored knotters over the natural knotters and tie 4 Square Knots.

Step 28: Bring the natural knotters over the colored knotters and tie 1 Square Knot.

Step 29: Bring the colored knotters over the natural knotters and tie 3 Square Knots.

Step 30: Bring the natural knotters over the colored knotters and tie 1 Square Knot.

Step 31: Bring the colored knotters over the natural knotters and tie 2 Square Knots.

Step 32: Pinch the colored knotters in with the natural carriers and use the natural knotters to tie 1 Square Knot over these 4 carriers.

Step 33: Cut the colored carriers so that the ends will be hidden in the following sinnet.

Step 34: Tie 6 more Square Knots.

Step 35: Tie a Switch Knot, which is about 1/2 inch long.

Step 36: Tie 7 Square Knots.

Step 37: Tie a Switch Knot, which is about 1/2 inch long.

Step 38: Tie 3 or 4 Square Knots (the same number used to begin the Slide Loop Clasp).

Step 39: If needed, continue tying Square Knots until the piece is the desired length. A "T" hook for an adjustable closure may also be added (See example and Page 24).

Step 40: To end, tie an Overhand Knot in each of the cords. Cut off the cords and add glue to each of the Overhand Knots. Any ending desired can be used to replace this step.

Celtic Luck Anklet

The length of the Sinnet in this piece (which is actually a Phish Bone using only two sets of knotters) can be adjusted before and after the Pretzel Knot and the piece worn as a choker.

Sample Length: 10 inches
Materials: (2) 4 foot lengths of 1.5mm natural hemp and (1) 3 foot length of 1mm colored hemp (turquoise in the example)

Step 1: Fold the two natural hemp cords in half and tie a Slide Loop Clasp. Finish with 4 Left Square Knots. Don't forget to tie a Half Knot in the carriers after the second or third of these Square Knots to secure the clasp.

Step 2: Add the 3 foot colored cord, centered across the existing carriers. Tie a Half Knot tight against the added cord (see Page 9).

Step 3: Pinch both sides of the new cord in with the existing bead carriers. Tie a second Half Knot to complete the Square Knot and secure the new colored carriers in position.

Step 4: Tie 1 more Left Square Knot over the 4 carriers (2 colored, 2 natural).

Step 5: Leave the natural knotters out to the side and use the colored hemp to tie 1 Left Square Knot over the 2 natural hemp carriers. There are now two sets of knotters (1 colored, 1 natural) and one set of carriers (natural).

Step 6: Put the colored knotters to either side. Bring the natural knotters over the colored knotters and tie 1 Left Square Knot. Put the natural knotters to the side.

Step 7: Bring the colored knotters over the natural knotters and tie 1 Left Square Knot.

Step 8: Alternate Steps 6 and 7 until 17 Left Square Knots have been tied, starting the count with the first colored knot and ending with a colored knot.

Step 9: Split the 6 cords into two sets of three cords. The colored cord should be in the middle of each set and the natural knotter to the outside. Use these two sets of cords to tie a tight Pretzel Knot snug against the last knot tied. Keep the cords parallel, with the colored one in the middle, in all portions of the knot to maintain the colored design.

Step 10: Divide the cords back into the previous three sets: natural knotters, colored knotters and natural carriers, in that order.

Step 11: Using the colored knotters, tie 1 Left Square Knot around the natural carriers.

Step 12: Alternate Steps 6 and 7 until 17 Left Square Knots have been tied, starting the count with the colored knot just tied and ending with a colored knot.

Step 13: Pinch the colored knotters in with the natural carriers and use the natural knotters to tie 1 Left Square Knot over these 4 carriers.

Step 14: Cut the shorter of the two sets of carriers (natural carriers in the example) so that the ends will be hidden in the next series of square knots.

Step 15: Tie 4 Left Square Knots with the natural knotters.

Step 16: Tie 1 Overhand Knot in each of the knotters to the side(s) of the last Square Knot. This creates a "T" hook to catch in the Slide Loop Clasp.

Step 17: Repeat Steps 15 and 16 until the desired length and number of "T" hooks have been reached.

Step 18: Tie an Overhand Knot in the carriers, snug below the last Square Knot. Cut all 4 cords and add glue to each of the ending Overhand Knots. Any ending desired can be used to replace Steps 16 through 18.

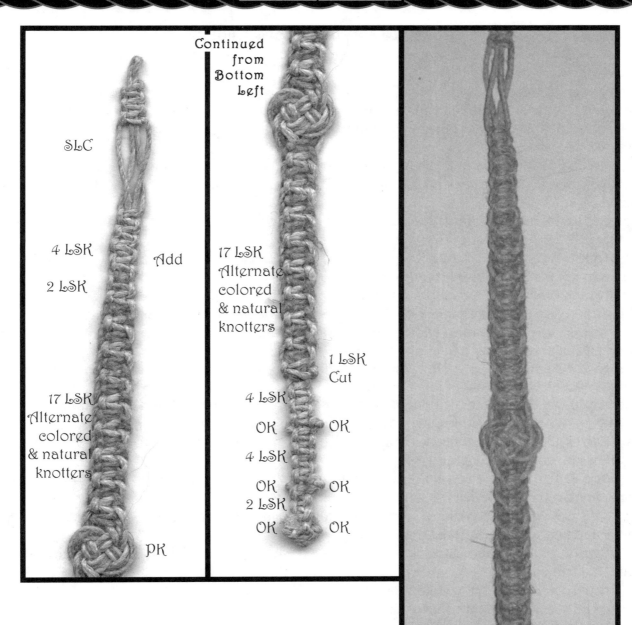

SLC

4 LSK   Add

2 LSK

17 LSK
Alternate
colored
& natural
knotters

PK

Continued
from
Bottom
Left

17 LSK
Alternate
colored
& natural
knotters

1 LSK
Cut

4 LSK

OK   OK

4 LSK

OK   OK

2 LSK

OK   OK

CELTIC LUCK ANKLET

Lucky 13 Celtic Colors Choker

This piece can be wrapped twice around the wrist and worn as a bracelet.

Sample Length: 16 1/2 inches

Materials: (1) 6 foot length of 1.5mm natural hemp, (1) 6 foot length of 1mm natural hemp and (1) 6 foot length of 1mm colored hemp (green in the example)

Step 1: Fold the two natural hemp cords in half. Start with the thin cords as knotters and tie a Slide Loop Clasp, starting with 3 Square Knots. Finish the Slide Loop Clasp with 7 Left Square Knots.

Step 2: Tie a Switch Knot, which is about a half inch in length.

Step 3: Tie 5 Right Square Knots.

Step 4: Add the 6 foot colored cord, centered across the existing carriers. Tie a Half Knot tight against the added cord (see Page 9).

Step 5: Pinch both sides of the new cord in with the existing bead carriers. Tie a second Half Knot to complete the Square Knot and to secure the new colored carriers in position.

Step 6: Leave the natural knotters out to the side and use the colored carriers to tie 1 Right Square Knot around the remaining natural carriers.

Step 7: Split the 6 cords into two sets of three cords. The colored cord should be in the middle of each set and the natural knotter (from Step 5) to the outside.

Step 8: Leave a space of about 1/8 inch in the cords and then tie a snug Pretzel Knot with the two sets of cords. (The knot in the example is slightly less than 3/4 of an inch wide and 1/2 inch long.) Keep the cords parallel, with the colored one in the middle, in all portions of the knot to maintain the colored design.

Step 9: Tie 12 more Pretzel Knots (for a total of 13), starting each Pretzel Knot on the opposite side from the previous knot tied to prevent the pattern from twisting. Adjust these knots so that they just barely touch one another and are fairly snug. The small spaces between the cords and knots are part of the design.

Step 10: Divide the cords back into the previous sets (2 natural knotters, 2 colored knotters and 2 natural carriers).

Step 11: Leave the natural knotters out to the side and use the colored cords to tie 1 Right Square Knot around the 2 natural carriers.

Step 12: Pinch the colored knotters in with the natural carriers and use the natural knotters to tie 1 Right Square Knot over these 4 carriers.

Step 13: Cut the colored carriers so that the ends will be hidden in the following sinnet.

Step 14: Tie 6 more Right Square Knots around the natural carriers and the cut colored carriers.

Step 15: Tie a Switch Knot, which is about a half inch in length.

Step 16: Tie 7 Left Square Knots.

Step 17: Repeat Steps 15 and 16 until the piece is the desired length. To end, cut the carriers, put glue on the cut ends and tie 1 last Square Knot over the glued ends. Tie an Overhand Knot in each of the knotters. Cut off the cords and add glue to each of these Overhand Knots.

Any ending desired can be used to replace Step 17.

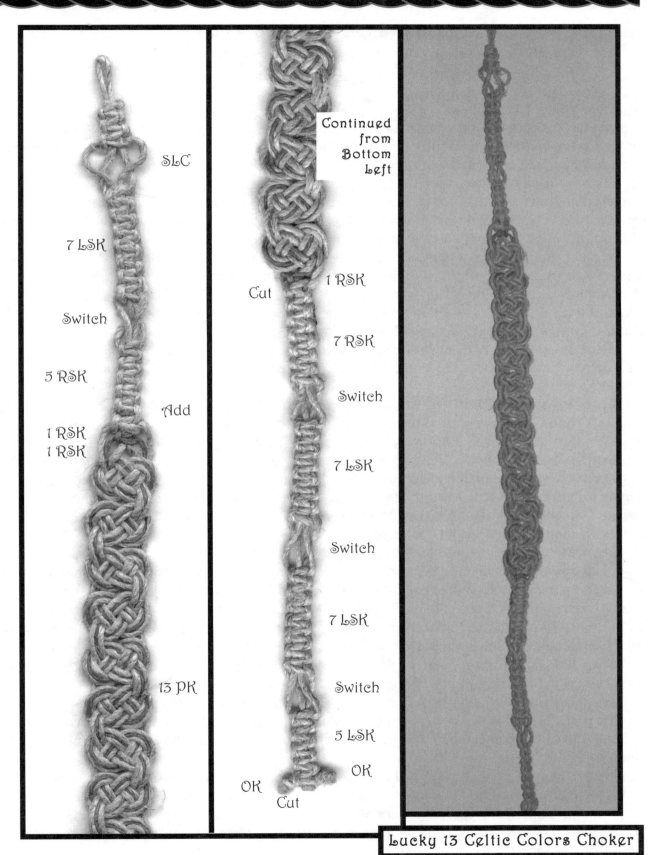

SLC

7 LSK

Switch

5 RSK

Add

1 RSK
1 RSK

13 PK

Continued
from
Bottom
Left

Cut

1 RSK

7 RSK

Switch

7 LSK

Switch

7 LSK

Switch

5 LSK

OK

OK

Cut

Lucky 13 Celtic Colors Choker

63

Color and Chrome Phish Bracelet

This piece can be lengthened before and after the Phish Bone and worn on
any part of the body.

Sample Length: 8 1/2 inches
Materials: (2) 4 foot lengths of 1.5mm natural hemp, (1) 3 foot length of 1mm colored hemp (black in the example), (1) 9 inch length of 0.5mm natural hemp and (1) 3/8 inch metal bead (chrome or nickel plate in the example)

Step 1: Fold the two 4 foot natural hemp cords in half and tie a Slide Loop Clasp. After the Switch, tie 3 Left Square Knots. Remember to tie a Half Knot or Overhand Knot in the carriers at this point, so they will not slide when the clasp is opened.

Step 2: Add the 9 inch length of thin natural hemp as a third carrier (in the center of the other two carriers; see page 8). At the same time, add the 3 foot colored cord, centered across the existing carriers. Tie a Half Knot tight against the added cords (see Page 9). Pinch both sides of the colored cord in with the three other carriers. Tie a second Half Knot to complete the Square Knot and secure the new colored carriers in position.

Step 3: Leave the natural knotters out to the side and use the colored hemp as knotters to tie 1 Left Square Knot over the 3 natural hemp carriers. There are now two sets of knotters and a set of 3 carriers.

Step 4: Put the colored knotters to either side. Use the remaining 1.5mm natural carriers to tie 1 Left Square Knot around the single remaining thin bead carrier. There are now three sets of knotters (first natural set, colored set, and second natural set) and a single thin bead carrier.

Step 5: Begin tying the Phish Bone pattern. To do this, bring the first (top) set of natural knotters over (in front of) the lower two sets of knotters. Tie a tight Left Square Knot around the single thin carrier (just below the last knot tied). This Phish Bone has loops which gradually increase in size so start with almost no slack in the knotters and remember to increase the loop size with each repetition of the pattern.

Step 6: Bring the colored knotters over (in front of) the two sets of natural knotters. Tie a tight Left Square Knot around the carrier, again leaving almost no slack in the colored knotters.

Step 7: Bring the second set of natural knotters over (in front of) the first two sets of knotters (1 colored and first natural). Check the size of the loops (same as in Steps 5 and 6) and tie a tight Left Square Knot around the carrier. Repetition of these three steps (5, 6 and 7) creates the Phish Bone effect; variations in loop size and bead placement make each piece unique.

Step 8: Repeat Steps 5, 6 and 7 three times. Increase the size of the knotter loops slightly with each repetition, ending with Phish Bones about 3/4 inch across.

Step 9: String the center metal bead on the thin bead carrier, snug against the last knot tied.

Step 10: Bring the bottom set of knotters (used to tie the knot just above the bead) around the outside of the center bead and tie 1 Left Square Knot around the carrier, snug below the bead.

Step 11: Flip the piece over (face down). This step is needed to make the second half of the pattern match the first half (a mirror image from the center point out to each end).

Step 12: Loop the colored knotters around (outside) the center bead and knots, go over (in front of) the previous knotters (from Step 10) and tie 1 Left Square Knot snug below the last knot.

Step 13: Loop the top set of natural knotters outside the colored center loops, go over the

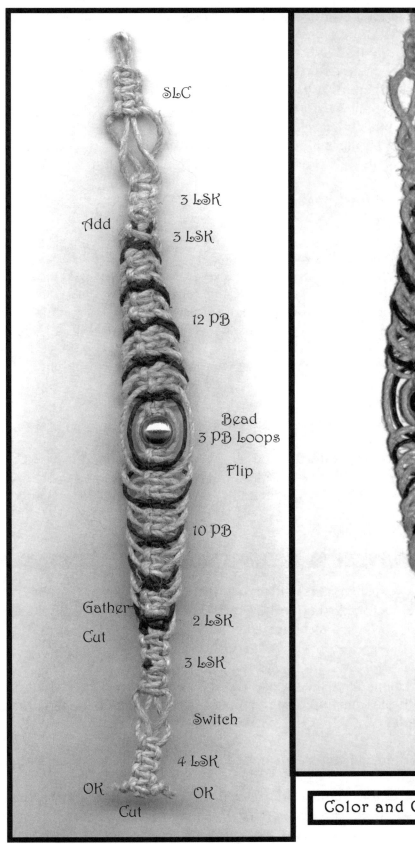

SLC

3 LSK

Add 3 LSK

12 PB

Bead
3 PB Loops

Flip

10 PB

Gather 2 LSK
Cut

3 LSK

Switch

4 LSK

OK OK
Cut

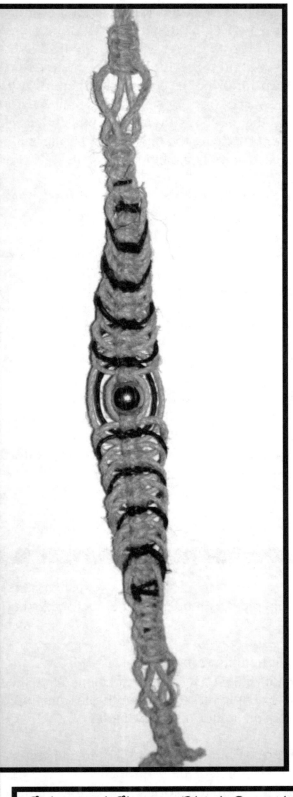

Color and Chrome Phish Bracelet

other two sets of knotters and tie 1 Left Square Knot snug below the colored knot just tied.

Step 14: Begin tying the Phish Bone pattern again. To do this, bring the top set of knotters (natural) over the other two sets and tie a Left Square Knot snug around the single thin carrier. Make sure that the loops are the same size as those tied just before the center bead was added.

Step 15: Bring the colored knotters over (in front of) the two sets of natural knotters. Check that the size of the loops match those tied before the center bead and tie a tight Left Square Knot around the carrier, snug beneath the last knot.

Step 16: Bring the third set of knotters (natural) over the other two sets of knotters. Check the loop size and tie a tight Left Square Knot around the carrier and snug beneath the last knot tied.

Step 17: Repeat Steps 14, 15 and 16 two times. Decrease the size of the knotter loops slightly with each repetition.

Step 18: Repeat Step 14.

Step 19: Pinch the natural knotters just used (in Step 18) in with the thin bead carrier and use the colored knotters to tie 1 Left Square Knot around these 3 carriers. Tie an Overhand Knot in the thin bead carrier to keep it from slipping and hide the knot under the next knot tied.

Step 20: Pinch the colored knotters in with the other carriers and use the remaining set of knotters (natural) to tie 1 Left Square Knot around all 5 carriers (2 colored, 2 natural, 1 thin natural).

Step 21: Cut the colored carriers and the thin natural carrier so that the ends will be hidden in the next Square Knot sinnet.

Step 22: Tie 3 Left Square Knots.

Step 23: Tie a Switch Knot which is 1/2 to 3/4 inch long.

Step 24: Tie 4 Left Square Knots.

Step 25: Repeat Steps 23 and 24 until the desired length has been reached. To end, cut the carriers, put glue on the cut ends and tie 1 last Square Knot over the glued ends. Tie an Overhand Knot in each of the knotters. Cut the cords and add glue to each of these Overhand Knots.

Any ending desired can be used to replace Step 25.

CHOKER ON PHISH COLORS
This piece can be shortened before and after the Phish Bone and worn as an anklet or armband.

Sample Length: 17 inches
Materials: (2) 6 foot lengths of 1.5mm natural hemp, (1) 4 foot length of 1mm colored hemp (white in the example), (1) 1 foot length of 0.5mm natural hemp and (7) 7mm crow beads (transparent light purple luster in the example

Step 1: Fold the two 6 foot natural hemp cords in half and tie a Slide Loop Clasp. After the Switch, tie 3 Left Square Knots.

Step 2: Add the 1 foot length of thin natural hemp as a third carrier (in the center of the other two carriers; see page 8). Tie 3 Left Square Knots, securing this new cord in position.

Step 3: Add the 2 foot colored cord, centered across the existing carriers. Tie a Half Knot

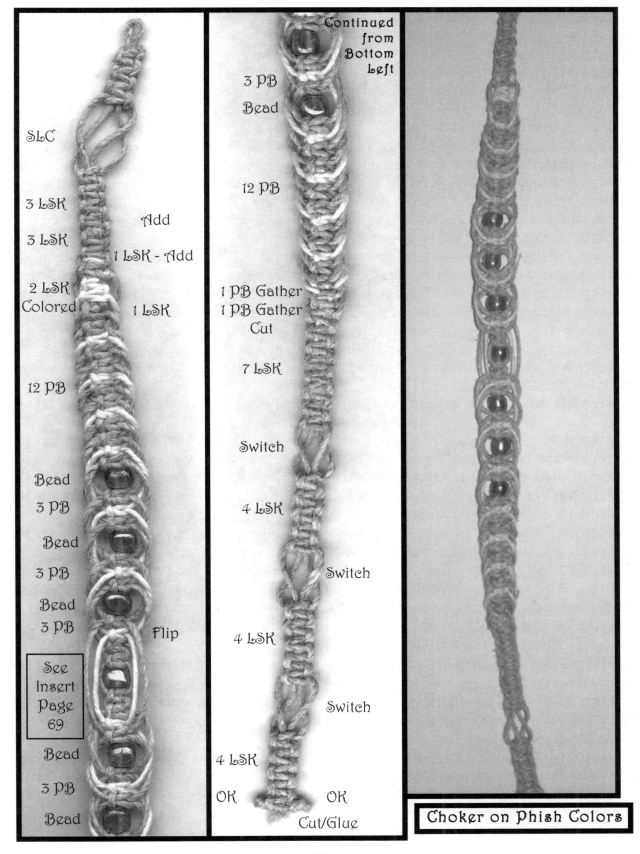

SLC

3 LSK

3 LSK   Add

2 LSK   1 LSK - Add
Colored   1 LSK

12 PB

Bead
3 PB

Bead
3 PB

Bead
3 PB   Flip

See
Insert
Page
69

Bead
3 PB

Bead

Continued
from
Bottom
Left

3 PB
Bead

12 PB

1 PB Gather
1 PB Gather
Cut

7 LSK

Switch

4 LSK

Switch

4 LSK

Switch

4 LSK

OK   OK
          Cut/Glue

Choker on Phish Colors

tight against the added cord (see Page 9). Pinch both sides of the new cord in with the carriers. Tie a second Half Knot to complete the Square Knot and secure the new colored carriers in position.

Step 4: Leave the natural knotters out to the side and use the colored hemp as knotters to tie 2 Left Square Knots over the 3 natural hemp carriers. There are now two sets of knotters and a set of 3 carriers.

Step 5: Put the colored knotters to either side. Use the remaining 1.5mm natural carriers to tie 1 Left Square Knot around the single remaining thin bead carrier. There are now three sets of knotters (first natural set, colored set, and second natural set) and a single thin bead carrier.

Step 6: Begin tying the Phish Bone pattern. To do this, bring the first (top) set of natural knotters over (in front of) the lower two sets of knotters. This is a tight Phish Bone so leave almost no slack in the knotters. Tie a tight Left Square Knot around the single thin carrier (just below the last knot tied).

Step 7: Bring the colored knotters over (in front of) the two sets of natural knotters. Tie a tight Left Square Knot around the carrier, again leaving almost no slack in the colored knotters.

Step 8: Bring the second set of natural knotters over (in front of) the first two sets of knotters (1 colored and first natural). Check the size of the loops (same as in Steps 6 and 7) and tie a tight Left Square Knot around the carrier. Repetition of these three steps (6, 7 and 8) creates the Phish Bone effect; variations in loop size and bead placement make each piece unique.

Step 9: Repeat Steps 6, 7 and 8 three times. Increase the size of the knotter loops slightly with each repetition.

Step 10: String the first bead on the thin natural bead carrier, snug against the last knot tied.

Step 11: Continuing the Phish Bone pattern, bring the first (top) set of natural knotters (from Step 6) around either side of the bead and tie 1 Left Square Knot snugly beneath the bead. Make sure that the loop size is the same or slightly larger than those in the Phish Bone section.

Step 12: Repeat Steps 7 and 8 (colored knotters, then the second set of natural knotters).

Step 13: String the second bead on the thin bead carrier and repeat Step 11.

Step 14: Repeat Steps 7 and 8 (colored knotters, then the second set of natural knotters).

Step 15: String the third bead on the thin bead carrier and repeat Step 11.

Step 16: Repeat Steps 7 and 8 (colored knotters, then the second set of natural knotters).

Step 17: Flip the piece over (face down). This step is needed to make the second half of the pattern match the first half (a mirror image from the center point out to each end).

Step 18: Use the bottom set of knotters (natural, the last ones used) and tie 1 more Left Square Knot around the single thin bead carrier.

Step 19: String the fourth (center) bead on the thin bead carrier, snug against the last knot tied.

Step 20: Bring the knotters from just above this new bead (the ones used in Step 18) around the outside of the bead and tie 2 Left Square Knots around the single carrier, snug below the center bead.

Step 21: Loop the colored knotters around (outside) the center bead and knots, go over (in front of) the previous knotters (from Step 20) and tie 1 Left Square Knot snug below the last knot.

Step 22: Loop the top set of natural knotters outside the colored center loops, go over the other two sets of knotters (natural, then colored) and tie 1 Left Square Knot snug below the colored knot just tied.

Step 23: String the fifth bead on the thin natural bead carrier, snug against the last knot tied.

Step 24: Begin tying the Phish Bone pattern again. To do this, bring the top set of knotters (natural) over the other two sets and tie a Left Square Knot snug beneath the bead. Make sure that the loops are the same size as those tied just before the center bead was added.

Step 25: Bring the colored knotters over (in front of) the two sets of natural knotters. Check that the size of the loops match those tied before the center bead and tie a tight Left Square Knot around the carrier, snug beneath the last knot.

Step 26: Bring the third set of knotters (natural) over the other two sets of knotters. Check the loop size and tie a tight Left Square Knot around the carrier and snug beneath the last knot tied.

Step 27: String the sixth bead on the thin bead carrier and repeat Step 24, again checking the loop size against the first half of the pattern.

Step 28: Repeat Steps 25 and 26, checking the loop size against the first half of the pattern.

Step 29: String the seventh and final bead on the thin bead carrier and repeat Step 24.

Step 30: Repeat Steps 25 and 26, checking the loop size against the first half of the pattern.

Step 31: Repeat Steps 24, 25 and 26 three more times. Decrease the size of the knotter loops slightly with each repetition.

Step 32: Repeat Step 24.

Step 33: Pinch the natural knotters just used (in Step 32) in with the thin bead carrier and use the colored knotters to tie 1 Left Square Knot around these 3 carriers.

Step 34: Pinch the colored knotters in with the other carriers and use the remaining set of knotters (natural) to tie 1 Left Square Knot around all 5 carriers (2 colored, 2 natural, 1 thin natural).

Step 35: Cut the colored carriers and the thin natural carrier so that the ends will be hidden in the next Square Knot sinnet.

Step 36: Tie 7 Left Square Knots with the remaining knotters.

Step 37: Tie a Switch Knot that is about a half inch long.

Step 38: Tie 4 Left Square Knots.

Step 39: Repeat Steps 37 and 38 until the desired length has been reached. To end, cut the carriers, put glue on the cut ends and tie 1 last Square Knot over the glued ends. Tie an Overhand Knot in each of the knotters. Cut the cords and add glue to each of these Overhand Knots.

Any ending desired can be used to replace Step 39.

Back Side of Center Section (As tied after Flip)
See Page 67

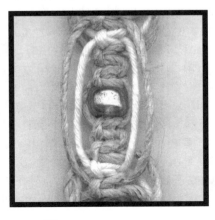

1 LSK

Bead

2 LSK

1 LSK Colored Loop

1 LSK Natural Loop

Colored Phish Bone Necklace with Beads and Charm

This piece can be shortened in length before and after the Phish Bone and worn as a choker.

Sample Length: 18 inches
Materials: (2) 7 foot lengths of 1.5mm natural hemp, (1) 2 foot length of 1mm colored hemp (purple in the example), (1) 1 foot length of 0.5 mm natural hemp, (6) 4 or 5mm pony/E beads (light purple luster in the example) and (1) 3/4 inch charm (gold filigree with a loop in the example)

Step 1: Fold the two 7 foot natural hemp cords in half and tie a Slide Loop Clasp. Finish with 7 Left Square Knots.

Step 2: Tie a Switch Knot that is about a half inch long.

Step 3: Tie 7 Left Square Knots (a flat sinnet).

Step 4: Tie a Switch Knot that is about a half inch long.

Step 5: Tie 3 Left Square Knots.

Step 6: Add the 2 foot colored cord, centered across the existing carriers. Tie a Half Knot tight against the added cord (see Page 9).

Step 7: Pinch both sides of the new cord in with the short bead carriers. Tie a second Half Knot to complete the Square Knot and secure the new colored carriers in position.

Step 8: Add the 1 foot length of thin natural hemp as a fifth carrier (in the center of the other two sets of carriers; see page 8). Tie 3 Left Square Knots around all 5 carriers (3 natural, 2 colored) to secure the new cords in place.

Step 9: Leave the natural knotters out to the side and use the colored hemp to tie 1 Left Square Knot over the 3 natural hemp carriers. There are now two sets of knotters and a set of 3 carriers.

Step 10: Put the colored knotters to either side. Use the remaining 1.5mm natural carriers to tie 1 Left Square Knot around the single remaining thin bead carrier. There are now three sets of knotters (first natural set, colored set, and second natural set) and a single thin bead carrier.

Step 11: Begin tying the Phish Bone pattern. To do this, bring the first (top) set of natural knotters over (in front of) the lower two sets of knotters. This is a very tight Phish Bone so leave almost no slack in the knotters. Tie a tight Left Square Knot around the single thin carrier (just below the last knot tied).

Step 12: Bring the colored knotters over (in front of) the two sets of natural knotters. Tie 1 Left Square Knot, making the loops of the Phish Bone the same size as the ones just tied.

Step 13: Bring the second set of natural knotters over (in front of) the first two sets of knotters (1 colored and first natural). Check the size of the loops and tie a tight Left Square Knot around the carrier. Repetition of these three steps (11, 12 and 13) creates the Phish Bone effect.

Step 14: Repeat Steps 11, 12 and 13 three times.

Step 15: String the first bead on the thin natural bead carrier, snug against the last knot tied.

Step 16: Continuing the Phish Bone pattern, bring the first set of natural knotters (from Step 11) around either side of the bead and tie 1 Left Square Knot snugly beneath the bead.

Step 17: Repeat Steps 12 and 13 (colored knotters, then the second set of natural knotters).

Step 18: String the second bead on the thin bead carrier, then repeat Step 16.

Step 19: Repeat Steps 12 and 13.

Step 20: String the third bead on the thin natural bead carrier, then repeat Step 16.

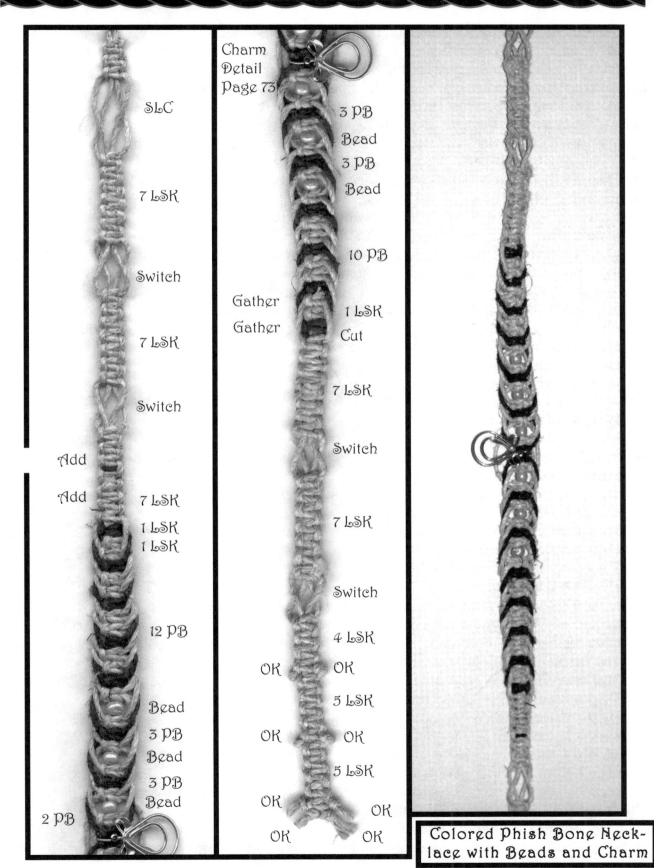

SLC

7 LSK

Switch

7 LSK

Switch

Add

Add   7 LSK

              1 LSK

              1 LSK

              12 PB

              Bead

              3 PB

              Bead

              3 PB

              Bead

2 PB

Charm
Detail
Page 73

                        3 PB

                        Bead

                        3 PB

                        Bead

                        10 PB

Gather   1 LSK

Gather   Cut

                        7 LSK

                        Switch

                        7 LSK

                        Switch

                        4 LSK

OK   OK

                        5 LSK

OK   OK

                        5 LSK

OK   OK

OK   OK

Colored Phish Bone Neck-
lace with Beads and Charm

71

Step 21: Repeat Step 12, which should be a colored knot.

Step 22: String the thin bead carrier and the left colored knotter through the loop on the charm. Bring the other colored knotter around the charm loop and tie 1 Left Square Knot snugly beneath the charm. (In the example a jump ring was attached to the charm and the cords strung through the jump ring so that the charm would hang properly. Other adjustments may be necessary depending on the type of charm used.)

Step 23: Flip the piece over (face down). This step is needed to make the second half of the pattern match the first half (a mirror image from the center point out to each end).

Step 24: Bring the knotters from below the third bead over the back of the charm and over the colored knotters. Leave some slack in these knotters so that they loop around the sides of the two center (colored) knots, then tie 1 Left Square Knot.

Step 25: String the fourth bead on the thin natural carrier, snug against the last knot tied.

Step 26: Bring the natural knotters from just above the third bead over the other two sets of knotters. Leave more slack in these knotters so that they form a fairly large loop around the outside of the previous knotters, then tie 1 Left Square Knot snug beneath the bead.

Step 27: Bring the colored knotters over (in front of) the two sets of natural knotters. Check that the size of the loops match those tied before the charm and tie a tight Left Square Knot.

Step 28: Bring the top set of natural knotters over (in front of) the other two sets (1 natural, 1 colored). Check the loop size and tie 1 Left Square Knot.

Step 29: String the fifth bead on the thin natural bead carrier. Bring the top set of knotters (natural) over the other two sets and tie a Left Square Knot snug beneath the bead.

Step 30: Repeat Steps 27 and 28.

Step 31: String the sixth and final bead on the thin natural bead carrier. Bring the top set of knotters (natural) over the other two sets and tie a Left Square Knot snug beneath the bead.

Step 32: Repeat Steps 27 and 28.

Step 33: Bring the top set of natural knotters over the other two sets of knotters. Check the loop size, and then tie 1 Left Square Knot.

Step 34: Repeat Steps 27 and 28.

Step 35: Repeat Step 33.

Step 36: Repeat Steps 27 and 28.

Step 37: Repeat Step 33.

Step 38: Pinch the natural knotters just used in with the thin carrier and use the colored knotters to tie 1 Left Square Knot around these 3 carriers.

Step 39: Pinch the colored knotters in with the other carriers and use the remaining knotters (natural) to tie 1 Left Square Knot around all 5 carriers (2 colored, 2 natural, 1 thin natural).

Step 40: Cut the colored and thin carriers so that the ends will be hidden in the next sinnet.

Step 41: Tie 6 more Left Square Knots with the remaining natural knotters.

Step 42: Tie a Switch Knot that is about a half-inch long.

Step 43: Tie 7 Left Square Knots.

Step 44: Tie another Switch Knot that is about a half inch long.

Step 45: Tie 4 Left Square Knots.

Step 46: Tie an Overhand Knot in each of the knotters to the side(s) of the last Square Knot. This creates a "T" hook to catch in the Slide Loop Clasp.

Step 47: Tie 5 Left Square Knots.

Step 48: Repeat Steps 46 and 47 until the desired length and number of "T" hooks have been reached. To end, tie an Overhand Knot in each of the cords. Cut off all four cords and add glue to each of the ending Overhand Knots. Any ending desired can be used to replace Steps 46 through 48.

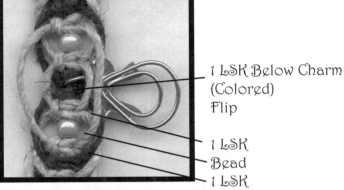

Back Side of Charm Section See Page 71

1 LSK Below Charm (Colored) Flip

1 LSK Bead 1 LSK

Froggy Phish Bone Necklace
Adjust the length of this piece on either side of the Phish Bone and wear it on practically any body part.

Sample Length: 17 1/2 inches
Materials: (2) 6 foot lengths of 1.5mm natural hemp, (1) 2 foot length of 1mm colored hemp (green in the example), (1) 1 foot length of 0.5 mm natural hemp and (1) 3/4 inch frog charm (pewter with a loop in the example)

Step 1: Fold the two 6 foot natural hemp cords in half and tie a Slide Loop Clasp. Finish with 7 Left Square Knots.
Step 2: Tie a Switch Knot that is about a half inch long.
Step 3: Tie 7 Left Square Knots (a flat sinnet).
Step 4: Add the 2 foot colored cord, centered across the existing carriers. Leave the ends of the new cords out to the sides to serve as a new set of knotters (see Page 9). At the same time, add the 1 foot length of thin natural hemp as a third carrier (in the center of the other two carriers; see page 8). Secure the new colored knotters and the new thin carrier in place by tying 1 Left Square Knot with the natural knotters from Step 3.
Step 5: Leave the original natural knotters out to the side and also bring the 1.5mm carriers out to the side as knotters. Use the new colored knotters to tie 2 Left Square Knots around the remaining single thin carrier. Leave the colored cords out to the side. There are now three sets of knotters (natural, natural and colored from top to bottom) and a single thin carrier.
Step 6: Begin tying the Phish Bone pattern. To do this, bring the first (top) set of natural knotters over (in front of) the lower two sets of knotters. Start with tight loops and leave almost no slack in the knotters. Tie a tight Left Square Knot around the single thin carrier (just below the last knot tied). The loops in this Phish Bone pattern increase in size to the center of the pattern and then decrease in a mirror image on the other side of the charm. (In the example the first loops are just under a half inch across and the loops on either side of the charm are just over three quarters of an inch wide.)
Step 7: Bring the second set of natural knotters over (in front of) the other two sets of

knotters (colored and natural). Tie a tight Left Square Knot around the carrier, making the loops of the Phish Bone slightly bigger than the ones just tied.

Step 8: Bring the colored knotters over (in front of) the first two sets of knotters (natural). Check the size of the loops (slightly larger again) and tie a tight Left Square Knot around the carrier. Repetition of these three steps (6, 7 and 8) creates the Phish Bone effect; variations in loop size make each piece unique.

Step 9: Repeat Steps 6, 7 and 8 five times, ending with a colored knot.

Step 10: Tie 1 more Left Square Knot with the colored knotters. Then string the charm on the thin carrier. Bring the colored knotters around either side of the charm loop and tie 2 Left Square Knots snugly beneath the charm. (In the example a link from pewter chain was attached to the charm and the cord strung through the link so that the charm would hang properly. Other adjustments may be necessary depending on the type of charm used.)

Step 11: Flip over the project. (Not you, flip the project face down.) This step is needed to make the second half of the pattern match the first half (a mirror image from the center point out to each end).

Step 12: Bring the middle set of knotters (natural) over the back of the charm and the colored knotters and tie 1 Left Square Knot. This is the first center loop of the Phish Bone and should be just a little wider than the first loops tied in Step 6.

Step 13: Bring the top set of knotters (natural) over the back of the charm and over the other two sets of knotters and tie 1 Left Square Knot. This is the longest and widest loop in the Phish Bone pattern. Use it to frame the charm.

Step 14: Continue tying the Phish Bone pattern. (If you are a whiz just tie the knots from the beginning to the center in reverse order and add an ending of your choice; if not, read on.) Bring the colored knotters over (in front of) the first two sets of knotters (natural). Check the size of the loops (slightly smaller this time) and tie a tight Left Square Knot around the carrier.

Step 15: Bring the top set of natural knotters over (in front of) the other two sets of knotters (natural and colored). Check the size of the loops (slightly smaller again) and tie a tight Left Square Knot around the carrier.

Step 16: Bring the second set of natural knotters over (in front of) the other two sets of knotters (colored and natural). Check the size of the loops (slightly smaller yet again) and tie a tight Left Square Knot around the carrier.

Step 17: Repeat Steps 14, 15 and 16 4 times.

Step 18: Repeat Step 14, but tie 2 Left Square Knots with the colored knotters.

Step 19: Gather the bottom knotters (colored) and the middle knotters (natural) in with the thin natural carrier. Use the top set of knotters (natural) to tie 1 Left Square Knot around the 5 carriers. Cut the colored carriers and the thin natural carrier so that the ends will be hidden in the remainder of this Square Knot sinnet.

Step 20: Tie 6 more Left Square Knots.

Step 21: Tie a Switch Knot that is about a half inch long.

Step 22: Tie 7 more Square Knots.

Step 23: Tie a Switch Knot that is about a half inch long.

Step 24: Tie 7 more Square Knots.

Step 25: Tie 1 Overhand Knot in each of the knotters to the side(s) of the last Square Knot. This creates a "T" hook to catch in the Slide Loop Clasp.

Step 26: Tie 5 Left Square Knots.

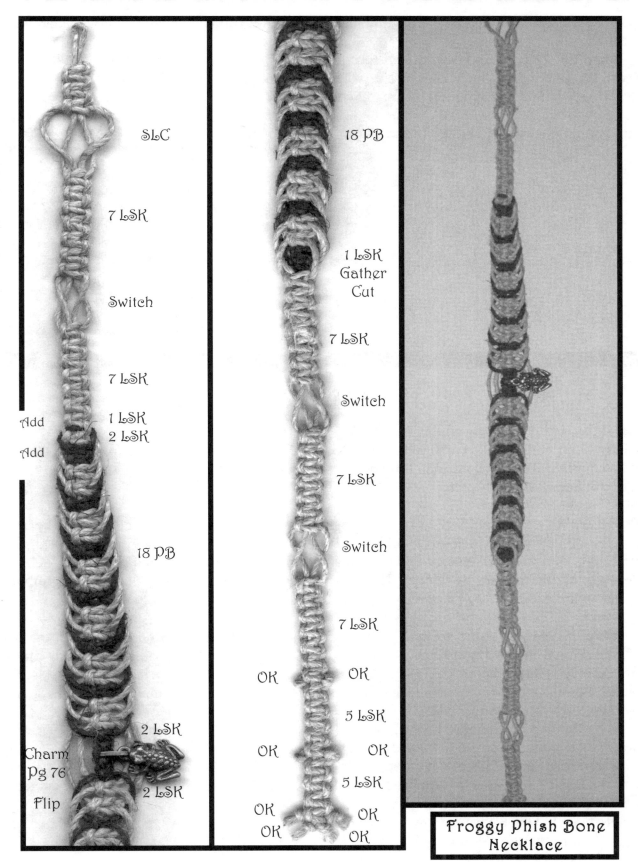

SLC

7 LSK

Switch

7 LSK

Add   1 LSK

Add   2 LSK

18 PB

2 LSK

Charm Pg 76   2 LSK

Flip

18 PB

1 LSK
Gather
Cut

7 LSK

Switch

7 LSK

Switch

7 LSK

OK   OK

5 LSK

OK   OK

5 LSK

OK   OK
OK   OK

Froggy Phish Bone Necklace

75

Step 27: Repeat Steps 25 and 26 until the desired length and number of "T" hooks have been reached.

Step 28: To end, tie an Overhand Knot in each of the carriers, snug below the last Square Knot. Tie an Overhand Knot in each of the knotters, to the sides of the last Square Knot. Cut off all four cords and add glue to each of the ending Overhand Knots.

Any ending desired can be used to replace Steps 25 through 28.

Back of Charm
See Page 75

2 PB Loops

Hempen Belt

Sample Length: 32 inches
Materials: (1) Belt Buckle, 1 inch wide, (4) 20 foot lengths of 1.5mm natural hemp, (1) 6 foot length of 1.5mm natural hemp, (11) 2 inch tube beads (red bamboo in the example), (20) 3/8 inch round beads (black wood in the example)

What a great looking belt! Red or black horn tubes or even antiqued bone hairpipe can be used in place of the bamboo for a different look. Round black horn beads are also available. Plan the length of the belt in advance and add an extra tube bead and two round beads for each two inches added to the sample length. The alternating knot tongue of the belt measures about 8 inches in the sample. Use longer cords if needed.

Step 1: Fold two of the 20-foot cords in half and mount them around one side of the belt buckle using a Lark's Head Knot (See Page 11). Do the same with the other two cords on the second side of the belt buckle. This gives four cords for knotting on each side of the buckle. The knotting on the left side of the buckle will be called Row A and the knotting on the right side of the buckle will be called Row B.

Step 2: Tie 4 Left Square Knots in Row A and 4 Left Square Knots in Row B. This secures the cords around the belt buckle and begins the pattern.

Step 3: Use the two knotters closest to the center of the belt (one from Row A and one from Row B) and tie 1 Left Square Knot between the two rows. This creates a third row in the center of the belt (Row C).

Step 4: Add the 6-foot cord as a carrier (see Page 8) in Row C and secure this cord by tying 3 Left Square Knots in Row C.

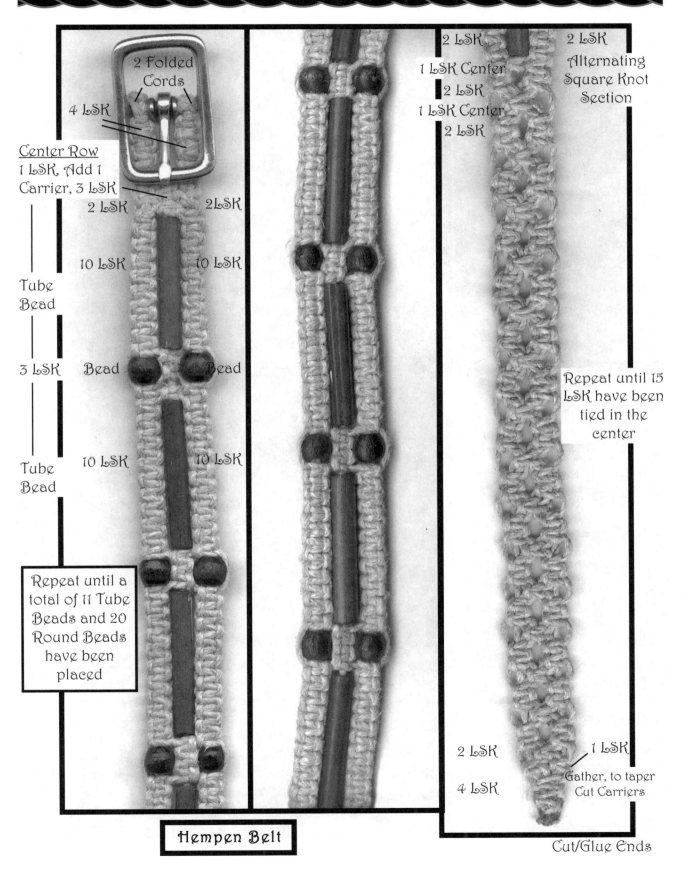

2 Folded
Cords

4 LSK

Center Row
1 LSK, Add 1
Carrier, 3 LSK

2 LSK   2LSK

10 LSK   10 LSK

Tube
Bead

3 LSK   Bead   Bead

Tube
Bead   10 LSK   10 LSK

Repeat until a
total of 11 Tube
Beads and 20
Round Beads
have been
placed

2 LSK   2 LSK

1 LSK Center

2 LSK

1 LSK Center

2 LSK

Alternating
Square Knot
Section

Repeat until 15
LSK have been
tied in the
center

2 LSK   1 LSK

4 LSK   Gather, to taper
                Cut Carriers

Hempen Belt

Cut/Glue Ends

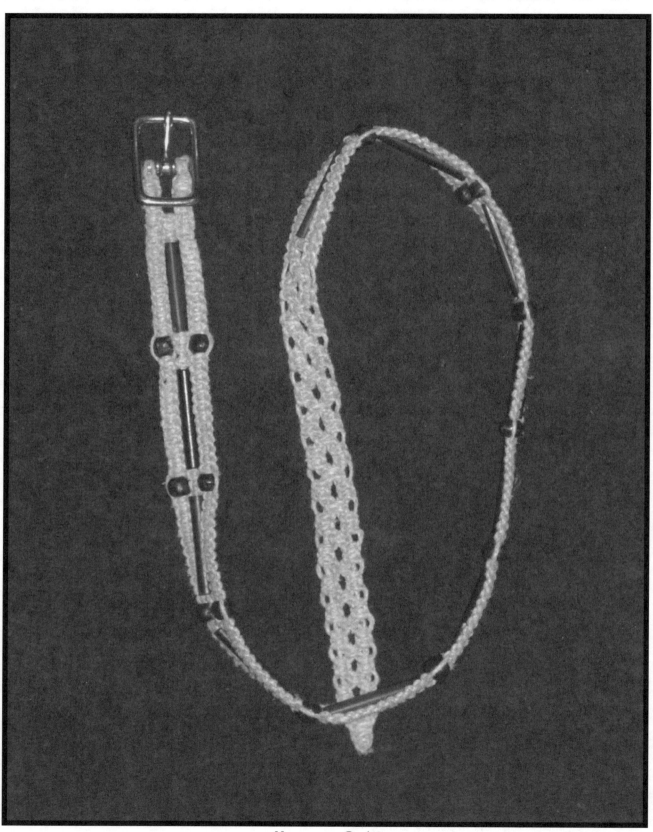

Hempen Belt

Step 5: Use the right bead carrier and the original left knotter in Row A to tie 2 Left Square Knots around the original left bead carrier in Row A.

Step 6: Use the left bead carrier and the original right knotter in Row B to tie 2 Left Square Knots around the original right bead carrier in Row B.

Step 7: Place a 2-inch tube bead on the bead carrier in Row C (center row).

Step 8: Gather the two knotters from Row C into Rows A and B (one knotter to each outside row).

Step 9: Tie 10 Left Square Knots in Rows A and B (around the two bead carriers).

Step 10: Use the two knotters closest to the center of the belt (one from Row A and one from Row B) and secure the tube bead in Row C by tying 3 Left Square Knots snug to the bottom of the bead.

Step 11: Thread a small round bead on the two bead carriers in Row A and another small round bead on the two bead carriers in Row B.

Step 12: Use the knotters from Step 10 (Row C) and the outside knotters in Rows A and B and tie 10 Left Square Knots in each row. Tie these sinnets snug against the bottom of the beads added in Step 11.

Step 13: Repeat Steps 7 through 12 until the bead pattern section of the belt is the length desired.

Step 14: Add a final tube bead to the carrier in Row C and repeat Step 10, but tie only 1 Left Square Knot.

Step 15: Gather the bead carrier from Row C in with the carriers from Row A. Use the left knotter from Row C and the outside knotter from Row A as knotters and tie 1 Left Square Knot. Tie an Overhand Knot in the bead carrier from Row C, then cut it so that the end will be hidden in the next knot and tie 1 more Left Square Knot.

Step 16: Use the right knotter from Row C and the outside knotter from Row B as knotters and tie 2 Left Square Knots in Row B to match those just tied in Row A.

Step 17: The rest of the belt is tied using the Alternating Square Knot technique (see Page 15). Set the outside cord from each row out to the side. Gather the remaining cords in the center; use the right carrier from Row A and the left carrier from Row B as knotters and tie 1 Left Square Knot in this center set.

Step 18: Split the cords from Step 17 back into two sets of four and tie 2 Left Square Knots in each set (two in Row A and two in Row B).

Step 19: Repeat Steps 17 and 18, 13 more times. Tie 1 LSK in Rows A & B the last time Step 18 is tied. More length can be added to the belt by repeating these steps additional times if desired.

Step 20: End this belt by gathering all the cords except the outside set (to be used as knotters) as carriers. Cut these carriers to graduated lengths so that they will be hidden in the following sinnet and so that this sinnet will taper to a point as fewer carriers are included. Plan for the tapering sinnet to be about 4 Left Square Knots in length. Cut the knotters and any remaining carriers snug to the last knot tied and saturate the ends with glue.

Spirit of America Flag

Sample Size: 11 1/2 inches by 7.675 inches
Materials: (1) 2 foot long flag pole or dowel about 0.25 inches in diameter, (12) 10 foot lengths of 1mm red hemp, (12) 10 foot lengths of 1mm white hemp, (24) 7 foot lengths of 1mm blue hemp, (14) 8 foot lengths of 1mm red hemp, (12) 8 foot lengths of 1mm white hemp and (50) 4 or 5mm white pony/E beads

The Spirit of American Hempy-ness: It is a well-known fact that Betsy Ross sewed the first American Flag out of red, white and blue pieces of hemp canvas; this was the common thread of the day. Now it is a well-known fact that Hemp Masters created the first American Hempy-ness Flag by tying 5340 alternating half knots. Can You Dig It!

To create American Hempy-ness you must be hip to the knotting style of alternating knotting. The flag is just that, a bunch of 2LSK's, alternating throughout the red and white stripes of the flag. The tricky part is the stars and the transition to the red and white stripes. (So if you must "Freak Out" do it away from anyone you know, it's an embarrassing display of bunk human emotion.) The stars are a combination of 2LSK's and 1LSK's with bead placement you must truly dig to create. The transition of blue hemp to red & white stripes is also a heavy Om you must dig to create.

So pay close attention,
You best read it twice,
For the Spirit of American Hempy-ness
Will make your bank nice!

Step 1: Fold two of the 10 foot red cords in half and place the flag pole through the loops created by the fold. These loops should be about 5.5 inches from what will be the bottom of the flag pole. Gather each set of cords together so that there are two knotters and two carriers. Tie 2 Left Square Knots (a sinnet) around each set of two bead carriers, snug to the flag pole. It is easiest to work with the flag pole across the top of the piece and knot from left to right (the bottom of the flag to the top).

Step 2: Repeat Step 1 with two more 10 foot red cords.

Step 3: Repeat Steps 1 and 2 using 10 foot white cords. Be sure the white cords are to the right of (above) the red cords on the flag pole.

Step 4: Slide the two red, knotted sinnets next to each other. Use the four center cords (one knotter and one carrier from each sinnet) as a new set of knotters/carriers and tie 2 Left Square Knots, using the Alternating Square Knot style (see Pages 15-17).

Step 5: Divide the eight red cords into two sets of four cords (to left and right of the center sinnet just tied) and tie 2 Left Square Knots in each set, just below the center sinnet.

Step 6: Repeat Step 4 with the white, knotted sinnets created in Step 3.

Note A: As the white stripe is tied, it must be attached to the red stripe on the left. This is true for all the stripes in the rest of the flag. Do this when going from one center sinnet to two edge sinnets. Before tying the two edge sinnets, thread the left knotter (white in this case) through the adjacent loop (red in this case) in the stripe to the left. The blue field is attached to

Spirit of America Flag - Figure 1

The star section is tied using 12 sets of 4 parallel cords, tied in one large ASK pattern. The sinnets are 2 LSK but the beads take the space of 1 LSK, requiring only one LSK in the rows containing beads, followed by a second row of one LSK each. See instructions for adding cords to tie the top six stripes.

Each stripe is tied using two sets of parallel cords. Use the alternating square knot pattern and tie two LSK at each junction.

Spirit of America Flag - Figure 2

Gather all of the cords at the end of each stripe and cut the carriers to graduated lengths.
Tie 4 LSK in each end creating a tapered sinnet.

the sixth stripe (white) in the same manner. For this to look good, all knots tied in the flag must be as close to the same size and snugness as possible.

Step 7: Repeat Step 5 with the white cords from Step 6. Thread the left-most knotter through the red loop on the right edge of the red stripe before tying these knots, as indicated in Note A.

Step 8: Repeat Steps 4 and 5 until you have a red stripe that is 11 inches in length. Leave the cords hanging loose and do not cut them at this time.

Step 9: Repeat Steps 6 and 7 until you have a white stripe that is 11 inches in length. This stripe should be attached to the red one, next to each center sinnet in the Alternating Square Knot pattern.

Step 10: Repeat Steps 1 through 9 to add two more stripes to the flag. Be sure to add each new set of cords to the right of the previous stripe. Then repeat Steps 1 through 9 again so that there are a total of 6 stripes, alternating red and white, each 11 inches long.

Step 11: Use the technique described in Step 1 to attach 12 groups of 7 foot blue cords (2 cords in each group) to the flag pole. Be sure all blue cords are to the right of the six stripes already tied. Tie 2 Left Square Knots (a sinnet) in each group, as described in Step 1.

Note B: The entire blue stars section is tied as one Alternating Square Knot pattern. That is, one row of knots is tied, from left to right, using all twelve groups of cords. Then the next row of knots is tied, starting back on the left edge. Don't forget to attach the blue section to the last white stripe, as described in Note A.

Step 12: Slide the blue, knotted sinnets close to one another and next to the white stripe (the right edge of the stars section should be about 1.5 inches from the top of the flag pole). Starting with the first two blue, knotted sinnets (on the left), use the four center cords (one knotter and one carrier from each sinnet) to tie 2 snug Left Square Knots. Then use the two right-hand cords from the second sinnet and the two left-hand cords from the third sinnet to tie 2 more snug Left Square Knots. Next use the two right-hand cords from the third sinnet and the two left-hand cords from the fourth sinnet and tie 2 more snug Left Square Knots. Continue in this manner until only the last two cords from the 12th sinnet remain untied.

Note C: There are now eleven sinnets in the pattern, each consisting of 2 Left Square Knots, with two extra cords on each side of the blue knotting section. To help keep track of them, these sinnets will be called A, B, C, D, E, F, G, H, I, J, and K from left to right, respectively.

Step 13: Place a white bead on the two bead carriers in sinnets B, D, F, H and J, snug to the last knot tied. In the next knotting sequence, each bead will take up the space of one Square Knot.

Step 14: Use the four cords closest to the white stripe (two extra and the two left-hand cords from sinnet A). Attach the left-most cord to the white stripe and tie 2 Left Square Knots snug to the last knot tied. Then use the two right-hand cords from sinnet A and the two left-hand cords from sinnet B (one will be a carrier from the bottom of the bead) and tie 1 Left Square Knot snug to the left and below the bead. Next use the two left-hand cords from sinnet A and the two right-hand cords from sinnet C (one will be the other carrier from the bottom of the bead) and tie 1 Left Square Knot snug to the right and below the bead. Continue in this manner until only four cords remain on the right edge of the blue section. Use these four cords (2 from sinnet J and two extra) and tie 2 Left Square Knots. Be sure all knots are snug.

Step 15: Return to the left side of the blue section. Leave the first two blue cords free. Use the next four cords and tie 1 Left Square Knot. Continue across the pattern, using the next four cords each time and tie 1 Left Square Knot in each set of four cords until there are just two extra cords remaining on the right side of the blue section.

Step 16: There are again eleven sinnets, this time consisting of 1 LSK each, with two extra cords on each side of the blue knotting section. Again designate these as A through J, from left to right. Place a white bead on the two bead carriers in sinnets C, E, G and I, snug to the last knot tied.

Step 17: Thread the far left knotter (extra cord) through the right loop in the white stripe. Use the first four cords (including the one threaded through the stripe) and tie 1 Left Square Knot snug to the last knot tied. Continue across the pattern, using the next four cords each time, and tie 1 Left Square Knot in each set of cords until the right edge of the pattern is reached. Some of the cords will have a bead threaded on them. Be sure all the knots are snug against either the previous knot tied or against the bead just added.

Step 18: Return to the left side of the blue section. Leave the first two blue cords free. Use the next four cords and tie 1 Left Square Knot. Continue across the pattern, using the next four cords each time and tie 1 Left Square Knot in each set of four cords until there are just two extra cords remaining on the right side of the blue section.

Step 19: Repeat Steps 13 through 18, four more times. This will result in 10 rows of beads set within the blue knotting pattern. There should also be eleven sinnets, consisting of 1 LSK each, with two extra cords on each side of the blue knotting section.

Step 20: Using the same designations of these sinnets, Repeat Step 13. Then repeat Step 17. This completes the Stars section - 50 in all!

Note D: The remainder of the stripes must now be added to the flag. While tying the seven remaining stripes make sure they are spaced evenly across the blue stars section. Each stripe is created in the same manner as those at the beginning of the flag, using 8 cords for tying. Also, each stripe must be attached to the stripe on its right. The tricky part is going from the 12 sinnets currently in the blue knotting section (A through K, from left to right, respectively) to the 14 sinnets needed to tie the rest of the stripes. What a concept!

Step 21: Add two of the 8-foot red cords centered across the carriers of blue sinnet A. Leave the red cords out to the sides and tie 1 Half Knot to secure them in place (see Page 9, Adding Cords). Gather all four blue cords and two of the red cords in as carriers. Cut all the blue cords so the ends will be hidden in the next two knots and use the remaining two red cords to tie 2 Left Square Knots around the gathered cords.

Step 22: Repeat Step 21 at blue sinnet B.

Step 23: Add two of the 8-foot white cords to blue sinnet C, repeating the instructions in

Step 21.

Step 24: Repeat Step 23 at blue sinnet D. Before tying the first of the Square Knots, place the center of one of the 8-foot red cords under the right white knotter and use the knot to secure it. Leave both ends of the red cord hanging to the right of the white sinnet as it is tied.

Step 25: Add <u>three</u> of the 8-foot red cords to blue sinnet E and secure them with a single Half Knot. Leave two of the red cords out to the left and secure the rest of the cords with 2 LSK as described in Step 21. (Say what? Read it again!)

Step 26: Use the two red cords from Step 24 and the two red cords hanging to the left from Step 25. Tie 3 Alternating Half Knots snug against the points where these cords were added on the right and left.

Step 27: Repeat Step 23 at blue sinnets F and G.

Step 28: Add <u>three</u> of the 8-foot red cords to blue sinnet H and secure them with a single Half Knot. Leave two of the red cords out to the right this time and secure the rest of the cords with 2 Left Square Knots as described in Step 21.

Step 29: Repeat Step 23 at blue sinnet I. Before tying the first of the Square Knots, place the center of one of the 8-foot red cords under the left white knotter and use the knot to secure it. Leave both ends of the red cord hanging to the right of the white sinnet as it is tied.

Step 30: Use the two red cords hanging to the right from Step 28 and the 2 remaining red cords from Step 29. Tie 3 Alternating Half Knots snug against the points where these cords were added on the right and left.

Step 31: Repeat Step 23 at blue sinnet J.

Step 32: Repeat Step 21 at blue sinnets K and L. There are now 14 sinnets to use in tying the remaining stripes. Ommmm . . .

Step 33: Complete the 7 remaining stripes in the same Alternating Knotting manner and to the same length as the first 6 stripes (see Steps 4 through 7). Don't forget to attach each stripe to the one on its left as the knots are tied.

Step 34: Make sure all 13 stripes are the same length. Add Left Square Knots as needed to accomplish this. Finish each stripe by gathering all the cords except the outside set (to be used as knotters) as carriers. Cut these carriers to graduated lengths so that they will be hidden in the following sinnet and so that this sinnet will taper to a point as fewer carriers are included. Plan for the tapering sinnet to be about 4 Left Square Knots in length and tie them. Cut the knotters and any remaining carriers snug to the last knot tied and saturate the ends with glue.

Congratulations! You have achieved The Spirit of American Hempy-ness!

Lacy, Red, White and Blue Bracelet

Sample Length: 10 inches
Materials: (2) 5 foot lengths of 1mm red colored hemp, (2) 5 foot lengths of 1mm white colored hemp and (2) 5 foot lengths of 1mm blue colored hemp

Attractive and patriotic, this piece can also be worn as an anklet. For a woman, this bracelet may need to be shortened. The centerpiece of this bracelet is a lacy alternating square knot section. Extend this lacy section to create a choker. What a concept!

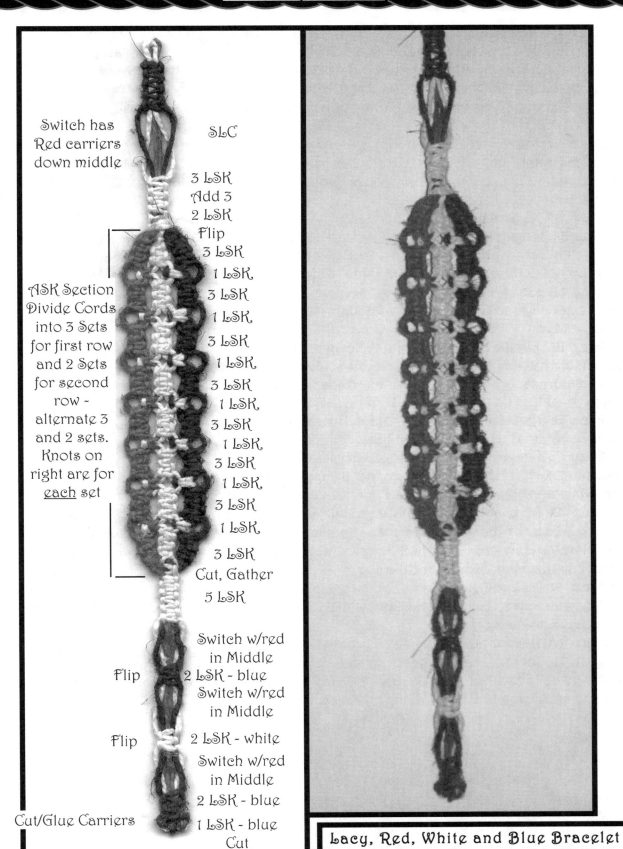

Switch has Red carriers down middle

SLC

3 LSK
Add 3
2 LSK
Flip
3 LSK
1 LSK
3 LSK
1 LSK
3 LSK
1 LSK
3 LSK
1 LSK
3 LSK
1 LSK
3 LSK
1 LSK
3 LSK
1 LSK
3 LSK

ASK Section Divide Cords into 3 Sets for first row and 2 Sets for second row ~ alternate 3 and 2 sets. Knots on right are for _each_ set

Cut, Gather
5 LSK

Switch w/red in Middle

Flip   2 LSK - blue
Switch w/red in Middle

Flip   2 LSK - white
Switch w/red in Middle
2 LSK - blue

Cut/Glue Carriers   1 LSK - blue
Cut

Lacy, Red, White and Blue Bracelet

85

Step 1: Fold three of the 5-foot colored hemp cords in half (one red, one white and one blue). Use the blue cords as knotters and tie a Slide Loop Clasp. At the Switch, bring the white cords out as knotters, bring the blue cords in as carriers and just let the red cords run down the center of the Switch as carriers. Tie 3 Left Square Knots with the white knotters. Remember to tie a Half Knot or Overhand Knot in the carriers at this point, so they will not slide when the clasp is opened.

Step 2: Add the remaining 5-foot colored cords centered across the carriers (see Page 9). Tie a Half Knot tight against the added cords, pinch the new cords in as carriers and tie a second Half Knot to complete the Square Knot. Tie 1 more Left Square Knot. Flip the piece over (face down).

Step 3: The center section of this piece is tied using the Alternating Square Knot technique (see Page 15). Split the cords, by color, into three sets of four cords each (4 red on the right, 4 white in the center and 4 blue on the left). Tie 3 Left Square Knots in each set of cords.

Step 4: Set the outside red cord aside to the right and the outside blue cord aside to the left. Split the remaining cords into two sets of five cords (3 colored and 2 white cords in each set). Use the outside cords in each set as knotters (1 colored and one white) and tie 1 Left Square Knot in each set.

Step 5: Split the cords back into the original three sets, as in Step 3. Leave enough slack in the outside red and blue cords (those set aside in Step 4) to create the lacy outside loops seen in the picture (about a quarter of an inch) and tie 3 Left Square Knots in each set (red, white and blue).

Step 6: Repeat Steps 4 and 5, 6 more times. This gives a total of 8 3-Square Knot sections for each color. Extend or shorten this section if desired. Can you dig it?!

Step 7: Gather all the cords together. Leave 2 cords of each color full length and cut the remaining cords (2 of each color) so that the ends will be hidden in this knotting sinnet. Use the long white cords as knotters and tie 5 Left Square Knots around the remaining cords.

Step 8: Tie a Switch Knot that is about a half inch long. Bring the white knotters in as carriers and bring the blue cords out as knotters. Leave the red cords running down the middle of the knot as carriers. Tie 2 Left Square Knots with the blue knotters to complete this Switch Knot. Flip the piece over (face down).

Step 9: Tie another Switch Knot, switching the blue and white cords and leaving the red cords as carriers. Complete this knot with 2 Left Square Knots, tied with the white cords. Flip the piece over (face down).

Step 10: Repeat Step 8.

Step 11: Cut the four carrier cords about a quarter inch below the last knot. Put some glue on the cut ends and tie a tight Square Knot around them with the blue cords. Cut the blue cords and add more glue to the end of the piece.

The USA Strong Arm Band

Sample Length: 12 inches

Materials: (3) 2 foot lengths of 1mm colored hemp (1 red, 1 white and 1 blue), (3) 6 inch lengths of 1mm colored hemp (1 red, 1 white and 1 blue), (2) 3 inch lengths of 1mm blue hemp, (2) 8 foot lengths of 1.5mm natural hemp, (1) 6 foot length of 1.5mm natural hemp and (2) 1 foot lengths of 1.5mm natural hemp

This pattern is one Heavy Bank Maker in any hempster's stringer. Creating the "USA Strong Arm Band" requires digging on the creative letter knotting style and some Heavy Hippie Meditation. It's a good idea to draw a pattern to use as a reference guide. The letters are made before creating the oval. It is necessary to plan out the points where the letters are going to attach to the oval and make attachment points as the letters are tied. Keep in mind that the knotted sinnets in the oval must be pulled very tight; this gives the oval a stiffness that is essential to successfully creating this piece.

Begin by creating the letters U in red, S in white and A in blue: To create any letter of the alphabet with hemp, Dig This! The sinnet must be bent to create the shape of the letter. To do this, one knotter must be pulled tighter than the other to make the sinnet bend naturally with the knotting. The tighter knotter must be the one opposite to the direction of the bend desired. That is, if the left knotter is pulled tighter than the right knotter, the sinnet will begin to bend to the right. As the sinnet of a letter is tied, keep in mind the shape and pull the knots snug, but not too tight, allowing the sinnet to bend. How a letter sinnet is begun and ended depends on where and how the letter will be attached to the rest of the piece. If the beginning is an attachment point, simply leave a carrier loop above the knotting to serve as an attachment point (fold the carrier cord so that the extra carrier ends after two or three knots). If the beginning is not an attachment point, fold the end of the carrier cord down after the first half knot and secure the end in the next one or two knots. If the end is an attachment point, a carrier can be looped with the end secured in the last few sinnet knots, or a length of carrier can be left hanging and secured later by gathering it into the knotting of the rest of the piece. If the end is not an attachment point cut all the cords snug to the last knot and place a drop of glue on the last knot.

The U:

Step 1: Fold the 2-foot red cord in half to serve as knotters. Fold the red 6-inch cord to serve as a carrier or filler cord, leaving a short loop in the top to serve as an attachment point later. The extra carrier should be short enough to end by about the third knot tied. Tie 11 Right Square Knots around the bead carrier. This knotting sequence will go to the bottom, middle of the U, so begin bending the sinnet to the right after the fourth or fifth knot. By the 11th knot the sinnet should be turned approximately 90 degrees.

Step 2: Leave a small loop in the outside (left) knotter, on the bottom side of the U. This will be used later to attach the bottom of the U to the bottom sinnet of the oval. Tie 11 more Right Square Knots, continuing to shape the U. The sinnet should be turned 180 degrees (parallel to the beginning arm) by the time the 6th or 7th knot in this step is tied.

Step 3: To finish, leave the carrier cord uncut (this cord will be used later to attach this end of the letter). Cut the knotters snug to the last knot tied and place a drop of glue on the cut ends and the last knot.

The S:

Step 4: Fold the 2-foot white cord in half to serve as knotters. Use the white 6-inch cord as a single carrier or filler cord, leaving just enough at the top to fold down after the first Half Knot and secure the end in the next one or two knots. Begin bending the sinnet to the right with the first knot (this is the top of the S). Tie 3 Left Square Knots.

Step 5: Leave a small loop in the outside (left) knotter, on the top side of the S. This will be used to attach the top of the S to the top sinnet of the oval, later in the pattern. Tie 13 Left Square Knots around the bead carrier, being sure to shape the S. Change the direction of the bend at about the 7th knot in this step.

Step 6: Leave a small loop in the outside (right) knotter, on the bottom side of the S. This will be used later to attach the bottom of the S to the bottom sinnet of the oval. Tie 9 Alternating Half Knots, continuing to bend the sinnet. Cut all the cords snug to the last knot and place a drop of glue on the cut ends.

The A:

Step 7: Fold the 2-foot blue cord in half to serve as knotters. Fold the blue 6-inch cord to serve as a carrier or filler cord, leaving a short loop in the top to serve as an attachment point later. The extra carrier should be short enough to end by about the third knot tied. This is the bottom of the left arm of the A and it is tied upside down. Tie 6 Left Square Knots. This sinnet does not need to be bent.

Step 8: Add one of the 3-inch lengths of blue cord, folded in half and the other as a single carrier. All three cords must lie on the left side of the sinnet. Before tying the cross of the A, remember that the left arm of the A will be on an angle and the cross piece needs to be horizontal. Tie 3 Left Square Knots in the new cords to create the cross of the A.

Step 9: Tie 4 Left Square Knots in the left arm of the A, securing the ends of the added cords.

Step 10: Leave a small loop in the outside (right) knotter, which will be at the top of the A. This loop will be used later to attach the top of the A to the top sinnet of the oval. Turn the left arm of the A right side up.

Step 11: To make the turn at the top of the A simply bend or turn the knotters and carriers around to a sixty degree angle from the left arm (visualize a triangle with three equal sides or use the reference pattern as a guide) and tie 4 Left Square Knots in the new direction.

Step 12: Gather the ends of the cords added in Step 8 into the sinnet of the right arm (as carriers). Cut them to end after two or three knots. Tie 6 Left Square Knots to complete the right arm of the A.

Step 13: To finish, leave the carrier cord uncut (this cord will be used later to attach this end of the letter). Cut the knotters snug to the last knot tied and place a drop of glue on the cut ends.

The Creation:

Step 14: Fold the two 8-foot natural cords in half and tie a Slide Loop Clasp. Finish the clasp with 3 Left Square Knots.

Step 15: Add the 6-foot natural cord, centered across the existing carriers. Tie a Half Knot tight against the added cord (see Page 9). Pinch both sides of the new cord in with the short bead carriers. Tie a second Half Knot to complete the Square Knot and secure the new cords in position.

Step 16: Split the 6 cords into two sets, 3 cords to a set. Tie 1 Left Square Knot in each set (sets A and B).

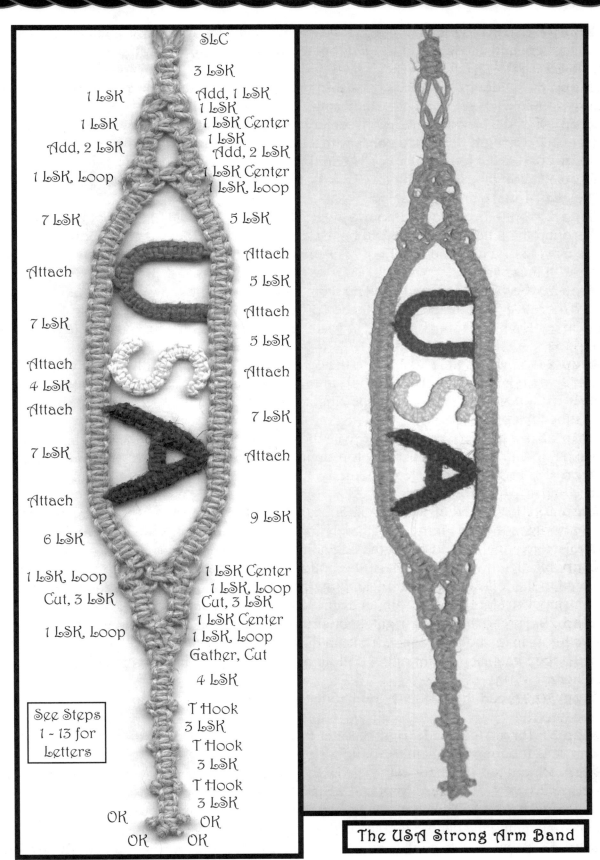

SLC

3 LSK

1 LSK   Add, 1 LSK
                1 LSK
1 LSK   1 LSK Center
                1 LSK
Add, 2 LSK   Add, 2 LSK

1 LSK, Loop   1 LSK Center
                1 LSK, Loop

7 LSK   5 LSK

                Attach
Attach
                5 LSK

7 LSK   Attach

                5 LSK
Attach
4 LSK   Attach

Attach   7 LSK

7 LSK   Attach

Attach   9 LSK

6 LSK

1 LSK, Loop   1 LSK Center
Cut, 3 LSK   1 LSK, Loop
                Cut, 3 LSK
                1 LSK Center
1 LSK, Loop   1 LSK, Loop
                Gather, Cut

                4 LSK

                T Hook
                3 LSK
                T Hook
                3 LSK
                T Hook
                3 LSK
OK   OK
     OK   OK

See Steps
1 - 13 for
Letters

The USA Strong Arm Band

89

Step 17: Use the four center cords (one knotter and the carrier from each sinnet) as a new set of knotters and carriers and tie 1 Left Square Knot, using the Alternating Square Knot style (see Pages 15-17).

Step 18: Divide the six cords back into two sets of 3 cords (Sets A and B) and tie 1 Left Square Knot in each set, just below the center knot from Step 17.

Step 19: Add a 1-foot natural cord, centered across the existing carrier (see Page 9) to each set (A and B). Secure the added cords with 2 Left Square Knots in each set.

Step 20: Use the four center cords and tie 1 Left Square Knot, as was done in Step 17.

Step 21: Using the remaining three cords in sets A and B (to either side of the knot in Step 20), tie 1 Left Square Knot in each set.

Step 22: Split the 10 cords into two sets of 5 cords. Set A will be the bottom sinnet of the oval around the letters and set B will be the top sinnet of the oval. Set the outside knotter of each set aside. Tie 1 Left Square Knot in each set, beginning to bend the sinnets away from the center with these knots.

Step 23: Gather the unused knotters from Step 22 back into their respective sets, leaving a small decorative loop in each. Use these cords as the outside knotters and tie 5 Left Square Knots in each sinnet (sets A and B). Remember to bend the sinnets outward (away from the center) to create the oval shape.

Step 24: Start tying the letters into the oval sinnets, beginning with the top sinnet. Thread the inside (left) knotter through the loop in the top of the left arm of the U. Tie 5 Left Square Knots in the top sinnet. Do not bend the sinnet any further; tie this section of the sinnet straight across the tops of the letters.

Step 25: Gather the uncut carrier from the right arm of the U into the top sinnet (as a carrier) and tie 5 Left Square Knots in the top sinnet, securing the carrier from the U in these knots.

Step 26: Thread the inside (left) knotter through the loop in the top of the S. Tie 7 Left Square Knots.

Step 27: Thread the inside (left) knotter through the loop in the top of the A. Tie 9 Left Square Knots in the top sinnet. Begin bending the sinnet back in towards the center after the 4th knot, matching the bend out at the beginning of this top sinnet.

Step 28: Begin tying the rest of the bottom sinnet, securing the bottom of the letters as indicated in the following steps. Picking up from Step 23, tie 2 more Left Square Knots in the bottom sinnet straightening the sinnet as these knots are tied.

Step 29: Thread the inside (right) knotter through the loop in the bottom of the U. Tie 7 Left Square Knots in the bottom sinnet. To keep the letters straight in the oval, it may be necessary to adjust the attachment point of the bottom of a letter by one knot to either side of that indicated here.

Step 30: Thread the inside (right) knotter through the bottom loop of the S and tie 4 Left Square Knots.

Step 31: Thread the inside (right) knotter through the bottom loop of the right arm of the A. Tie 7 more Left Square Knots in the bottom sinnet.

Step 32: Gather the uncut carrier from the right arm of the A into the bottom sinnet (as a carrier) and tie 6 Left Square Knots, securing the carrier from the A in these knots (cut the carrier to end before the 5th knot). Begin bending the sinnet back in towards the center after the first knot, matching the bend out at the beginning of this bottom sinnet.

Step 33: Bring the two sinnets together. Use the four center cords as a new set of knotters/

carriers and tie 1 Left Square Knot.

Step 34: Set the outside knotter of each sinnet (sets A and B) aside. Tie 1 Left Square Knot in the remaining two cords of each set, to either side of the center knot tied in Step 33.

Step 35: Gather the unused knotters from Step 34 back into their respective sets (A and B), leaving a small decorative loop in each. Use these cords as the outside knotters. Cut two of the carriers in each set to end in the next three knots and tie 3 Left Square Knots in each sinnet.

Step 36: Use the four center cords as a new set of knotters/carriers and tie 1 Left Square Knot. Leave the outside knotters to the side.

Step 37: Gather the unused knotters from Step 36 back into their respective sets (A and B), leaving a small decorative loop in each. Use these cords as the outside knotters and tie 1 Left Square Knot in each set.

Step 38: Gather all six cords together into one set. Cut two of the carriers to end in the next three knots and tie 4 Left Square Knots around the gathered cords.

Step 39: Finish this armband by tying Square Knots to the length desired and using any of the ending knots on Pages 24 and 25. The author tied a "T hook" after Step 38, followed by 3 Left Square Knots. This was repeated twice more, then an Overhand Knot was tied in each cord, the cords were cut and glue applied to each ending knot.

The Proud American Mirror Charm

Sample Size: 5 inches by 12 inches
Materials: (3) 6 foot lengths of 1mm colored hemp (1 red, 1 white and 1 blue), (2) 7 inch lengths of 1mm blue hemp, (11) 1 foot lengths of 1.5mm natural hemp (filler cords) and (2) 10 foot lengths of 1.5mm natural hemp

To create the "Proud American" a hempster must dig on the creative letter knotting style and do some Heavy Hippie Meditation. It's a good idea to draw a pattern to use as a reference guide. The letters are made and attached to each other before creating the mirror charm circle. It is necessary to plan out the points where the letters are going to attach to each other and the circle and make attachment points as the letters are tied. Keep in mind that the knotted sinnets in the circle must be pulled very tight; this gives the circle a stiffness that is essential to successfully creating this piece.

Begin by creating the letters U in red, S in white and A in blue:
To create any letter of the alphabet with hemp, the sinnet must be bent to create the shape of the letter. To do this, one knotter must be pulled tighter than the other to make the sinnet bend naturally with the knotting. The tighter knotter must be the one opposite to the direction of the bend desired. That is, if the left knotter is pulled tighter than the right knotter, the sinnet will begin to bend to the right. As the sinnet of a letter is tied, keep in mind the shape and pull the knots snug, but not too tight, allowing the sinnet to bend. How a letter sinnet is begun and ended depends on where and how the letter will be attached to the rest of the piece. If either end is an attachment point, a carrier loop can be secured in the knotting of the sinnet or a length of carrier can be left hanging for attachment in the knotting of the rest of the pattern. If the ends are not attachment points, the end of a carrier cord can be looped back up into the knotting or

it can be cut and glued. Knotters at the end of a letter should be cut snug to the last knot and glue put on the cut ends.

The U:

Step 1: Fold the 6-foot red cord and one of the 1-foot natural cords in half. Use the red cords as knotters and the natural cords as carriers. Leave about 3/4 inch of the carrier loop at the top as an attachment point. Tie 12 Left Square Knots around the carriers. Notice how this sinnet must flex when it is attached to the circle so tie the knots snug, but not too tight.

Step 2: Leave a small loop in the outside (left) knotter, on the side of the U. This will be used to attach the side of the U to the circle. Tie 11 more Left Square Knots.

Step 3: Leave a small attachment loop in the outside (left) knotter, on the side of the U (2nd attachment point). Create the bottom of the U by tying 5 Left Square Knots, turning the sinnet sharply (180 degrees) as the knots are tied. With this turn the U is now being tied upside down.

Step 4: Leave a small attachment loop in the outside (left) knotter, on the side of the U (to attach to the end of the S). Tie 23 Left Square Knots, creating the flexible right arm of the U.

Step 5: Leave a small attachment loop in the outside (left) knotter, on the side of the U (to attach to the top half of the S). Tie 5 left Square Knots to finish the right arm.

Step 6: To finish, leave a carrier cord uncut (to attach to the circle). Cut the remaining carrier and the knotters snug to the last knot and place a drop of glue on the cut ends.

The S:

Step 7: Fold the 6-foot white cord and one of the 1-foot natural cords in half. Use the white cords as knotters and the natural cords as carriers. Leave about 3/4 inch of the carrier loop at the top as an attachment point. Begin bending the sinnet to the right with the first knot (this is the top of the S). Tie 8 Left Square Knots around the carriers.

Step 8: Leave a small attachment loop in the outside (left) knotter, on the top of the S (to attach to the circle). Tie 10 Left Square Knots around the carrier, continuing to shape the top curve of the S.

Step 9: Thread the left knotter through the loop on the upper right arm of the U (see Step 5) and tie 30 Left Square Knots. Change the direction of the bend in the S at about the 13th knot in this step.

Step 10: Leave a small attachment loop in the outside (right) knotter (to attach to the bottom of the A). Tie 12 Left Square Knots, continuing to shape the bottom curve of the S.

Step 11: Leave a small loop in the outside (right) knotter, on the bottom side of the S (to attach to the circle). Tie 7 Left Square Knots, continuing to bend the sinnet.

Step 12: Cut one of the carriers snug to the last knot tied. Thread the remaining carrier through the loop in the U created in Step 4. Fold the carrier back into the sinnet of the S, leaving about a quarter of an inch between the U and the S. Tie 1 Alternating Half Knot to secure the folded carrier. Cut the folded carrier snug to this knot. Tie 3 more Alternating Half Knots to complete the S.

Step 13: Cut the knotters snug to the last knot tied and place a drop of glue on the cut ends.

The A:

Step 14: Fold the 6-foot blue cord and one of the 1-foot natural cords in half. Use the blue cords as knotters and the natural cords as carriers. Leave about 3/4 inch of the carrier loop at the top as an attachment point. Tie 12 Left Square Knots (blue) around the carriers. This is the bottom of the right arm of the A and it is tied upside down. This sinnet must also flex when it is attached to the circle, so tie the knots snug, but not too tight.

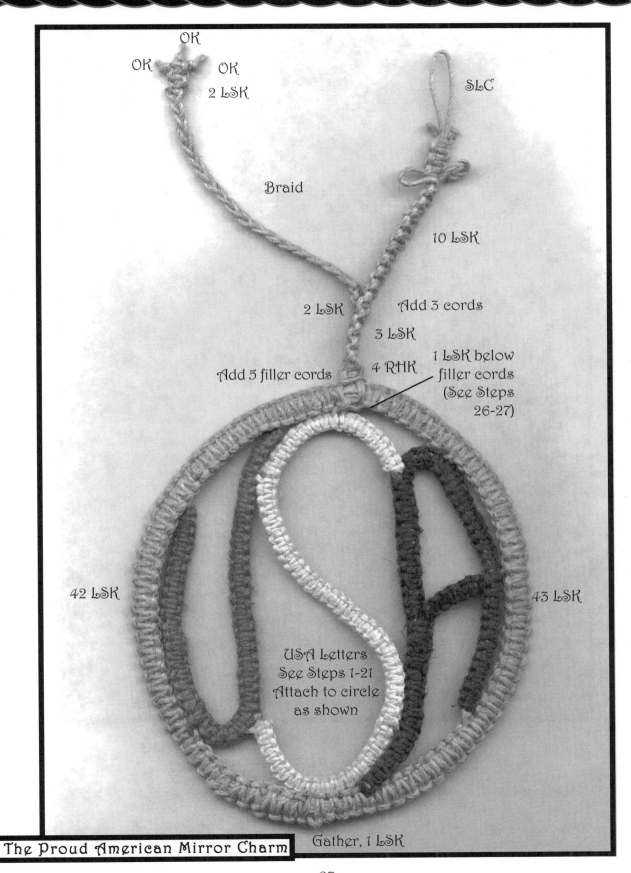

OK

OK   OK

2 LSK

SLC

Braid

10 LSK

2 LSK   Add 3 cords

3 LSK

Add 5 filler cords   4 RHK   1 LSK below
filler cords
(See Steps
26-27)

42 LSK   43 LSK

USA Letters
See Steps 1-21
Attach to circle
as shown

Gather, 1 LSK

The Proud American Mirror Charm

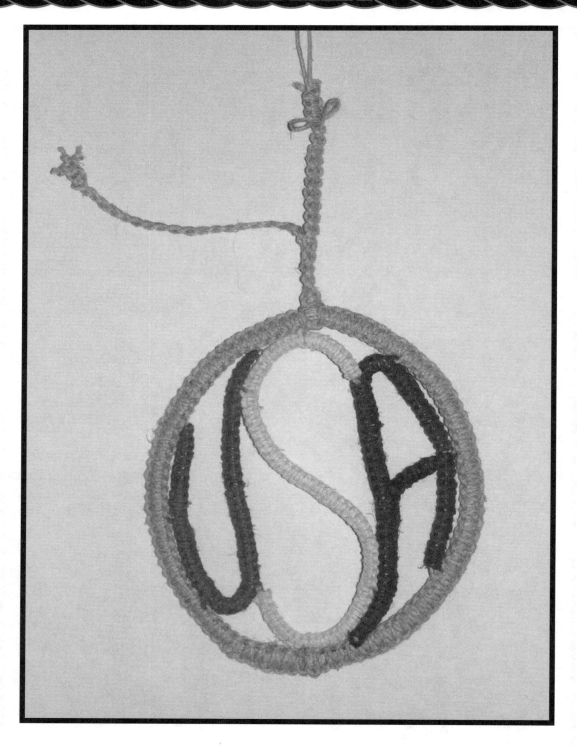

The Proud American Mirror Charm

Step 15: Add the two 7-inch lengths of blue cord, folded in half around the carriers so that the cords lay to the right side of the sinnet. Tie 6 Left Square Knots in the new cords to create the cross in the A. Leave the cords hanging for attachment on the other side of the A.

Step 16: Leave a small attachment loop in the outside (left) knotter on the side of the A (to attach to the circle). Remember that this arm (right) of the A is being tied upside down. Tie 11 Left Square Knots.

Step 17: Leave a small attachment loop in the outside (left) knotter, on the side of the A (2nd attachment point to the circle). Create the rounded top of the A by tying 4 Left Square Knots, turning the sinnet sharply (180 degrees) as the knots are tied. With this turn the A is now being tied right side up.

Step 18: Gather the carrier loop from the top end of the S into the sinnet of the A (as carriers). Cut the S carriers to end in the next two or three knots. Tie 12 Left Square Knots in the left arm of the A, securing the carriers from the S.

Step 19: Gather the cords from the cross in the A (see Step 15) into the arm sinnet of the A (as carriers). Cut all four of these cords to end in the next three or four knots. Tie 10 Left Square Knots in the left arm of the A, securing the cords from the cross.

Step 20: Thread the left knotter through the loop in the S created in Step 10 and pull the S snug against the A. Tie 6 Left Square Knots to finish the left arm of the A.

Step 21: To finish, leave a carrier cord uncut (to attach this end to the circle). Cut the remaining carrier and the knotters snug to the last knot and place a drop of glue on the cut ends.

The Circle and Letter Attachment:

Step 22: Fold the two 10-foot natural cords in half and tie a Slide Loop Clasp. Finish the clasp with 10 Left Square Knots.

Step 23: Add three of the 1-foot natural cords, as if they were new carriers (see Page 8) but upside down, so that the long ends are out in front of the main sinnet (not to the sides) and only the short (1 inch) ends are in position to be tied into the main sinnet. Leave the new cords out to the front and secure the ends by tying 3 Left Square Knots with the original knotters and carriers. The new cords will become the second half of the mirror clasp.

Step 24: Using the new cords from Step 24, tie 2 Left Square Knots. Then Braid (see Page 30) these cords until this section is long enough to reach the top of the Slide Loop Clasp (about 3 1/2 inches). Tie 2 more Left Square Knots, then tie an Overhand Knot in each of the cords, cut the cords and put of drop of glue on the cut ends. This creates an end which can secured in the Slide Loop Clasp.

Step 25: Return to the original knotters and carriers and tie 4 Right Half Knots, giving the sinnet a half twist so that the circle will hang properly.

Step 26: Add the remaining five 1-foot natural cords across the center of the existing carriers. Tie a Half Knot tight against the added cord (see Page 9). Leave the new cords out to the sides (these are filler cords for the circle). Tie a second Half Knot to complete the Square Knot and secure the new cords in position.

Step 27: Leave the original knotters out to the side, below the filler cords. Use the original carriers as knotters. Bring these carriers up, behind the filler cords and tie 1 Left Square Knot around the original sinnet, above the filler cords. This creates two new sets of knotters, one for each side of the circle. Each set consists of one original knotter (below the filler cords) and one original carrier (above the filler cords). The circle is created by tying square knots around the filler cords, as explained in the following steps. Tie each side of the circle from top to bottom.

Tie the left side first, then the right side. Note: Since all knotters have their own style, it may be necessary to adjust some of the letter-circle attachment points by one or two knots to either side of the position indicated in these instructions.

Step 28: On the left side of the circle, tie an Alternating Half Knot around the filler cords. Thread the right (inside) knotter through the loop in the top of the S (Step 8) and tie another Alternating Half Knot.

Step 29: Cut the carrier at the top of the right arm of the U (Step 6) to about 3/4 of an inch. Lay the cut end in with the filler cords below the last knot tied. Tie 4 Left Square Knots around the filler cords and the U carrier, securing the top, right of the U in position. Begin bending the sinnet into a semi-circle.

Step 30: Tie 6 Left Square Knots around the filler cords. Continue bending the sinnet.

Step 31: Lay the top carrier loop from the left arm of the U (Step 1) in with the filler cords below the last knot tied. Tie 4 Left Square Knots around the filler cords and the U carrier loop, securing the top, left of the U in position.

Step 32: Tie 10 Left Square Knots around the filler cords. Don't forget to bend the sinnet.

Step 33: Thread the right (inside) knotter through the loop in the side of the U (Step 2) and tie 9 Left Square Knots. Continue bending the sinnet.

Step 34: Thread the right (inside) knotter through the second loop in the side of the U (Step 3) and tie 8 Left Square Knots. Finish bending the sinnet as these knots are tied.

Step 35: Return to the top of the circle and tie 7 Left Square Knots around the filler cords on the right side of the circle. Begin bending the sinnet into a semi-circle as these knots are tied.

Step 36: Thread the left (inside) knotter through the loop near the top of the A (Step 17) and tie 11 Left Square Knots. Continue bending the sinnet.

Step 37: Thread the left (inside) knotter through the loop in the side of the A (Step 16) and tie 12 Left Square Knots. Continue bending the sinnet.

Step 38: Gather the bottom carrier loop from the right arm of the A (Step 14) in with the filler cords. Tie 9 Left Square Knots around the filler cords and the A carrier loop, securing the bottom, right of the A in position. Continue bending the sinnet.

Step 39: Gather the carrier from the bottom of the left arm of the A (Step 21) in with the filler cords. Cut the carrier to end within the next two or three knots. Tie 3 Left Square Knots around the filler cords and the A carrier, securing the bottom, left of the A in position. Continue bending the sinnet.

Step 40: Thread the left (inside) knotter through the loop in the bottom of the S (Step 11) and tie 1 Left Square Knot.

Step 41: Gather the right side knotters in with the filler cords. Cut the filler cords (including the right side knotters) on both sides of the circle and butt the ends against one another (interlace them slightly). Place a drop of glue on the interlaced ends. Use the knotters from the left side of the circle and secure this connection with 1 Left Square Knot. Cut the left side knotters close to the last knot tied and place a drop of glue on the cut ends. Finito!

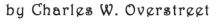
PLAINS INDIAN And MOUNTAIN MAN ARTS & CRAFTS
by Charles W. Overstreet

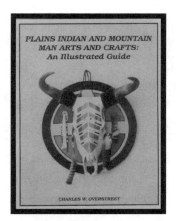

This illustrated handbook is an exciting exploration of the arts, crafts and accoutrements made and used by the Plains Indians and Mountain Men in the early 1800's. Employing traditional and modern methods, this complete how-to manual features 45 projects ranging from rawhide to an Arapaho saddle. Using the easy-to-follow instructions and illustrations, re-creation of these historical items becomes a simple task. A varied selection of items that can be made relatively inexpensively is provided. The author provides interesting historical background on the use and significance of each piece.

CLASSIC EARRING DESIGNS
by Nola May

No wonder beading is so popular! It's easy to learn, and creating beautiful personalized accessories is a very satisfying experience. This collection of Comanche Weave (or Brick Stitch) earring designs has color combinations inspired by Mother Nature herself. Aimed at beginning and intermediate beaders, this book has 52 new and exciting patterns that are sure to stimulate the creativity of advanced beaders as well. There are easy-to-follow instructions, lots of illustrations and sections on materials, techniques, basic earring patterns, and variations on the basic designs. A great way to learn how to bead!

TECHNIQUES OF NORTH AMERICAN INDIAN BEADWORK
by Monte Smith

This informative, easy to read book contains complete instructions on every facet of beadwork. Included is information on selecting beads; materials and their use; designs; making looms and loomwork; applique stitches such as the lazy, "crow", running, spot and return stitches; bead wrapping and peyote stitch; making rosettes and beaded necklaces; and beadwork edging. There is a selected bibliography and an index. The book features examples and photos of beadwork from 1835 to the present time from 23 tribes. Anyone interested in Native American craftwork will profit from owning this book.

SOME EAGLE'S VIEW BESTSELLERS THAT MAY BE OF INTEREST:

❑ Eagle's View Publishing Catalog of Books	BOO/00	$4.00
❑ The Technique of Porcupine Quill Decoration/Orchard	BOO/01	$9.95
❑ The Technique of North American Indian Beadwork/Smith	BOO/02	$13.95
❑ Techniques of Beading Earrings by Deon DeLange	BOO/03	$9.95
❑ More Techniques of Beading Earrings by Deon DeLange	BOO/04	$9.95
❑ Traditional Clothing of the Native Americans by Evard Gibby	BOO/05	$17.95
❑ Crow Indian Beadwork/Wildschut and Ewers	BOO/06	$10.95
❑ New Adventures in Beading Earrings by Laura Reid	BOO/07	$9.95
❑ The Beading of My Heart by Mary Thompson	BOO/09	$15.95
❑ Traditional Indian Crafts by Monte Smith	BOO/10	$12.95
❑ Traditional Indian Bead & Leather Crafts/ Smith/VanSickle	BOO/11	$9.95
❑ Indian Clothing of the Great Lakes: 1740-1840/Hartman	BOO/12	$14.95
❑ Shinin' Trails: A Possibles Bag of Fur Trade Trivia by Legg	BOO/13	$8.95
❑ Adventures in Creating Earrings by Laura Reid	BOO/14	$9.95
❑ Circle of Power by William Higbie	BOO/15	$8.95
❑ Etienne Provost: Man of the Mountains by Jack Tykal	BOO/16	$9.95
❑ A Quillwork Companion by Jean Heinbuch	BOO/17	$12.95
❑ Making Indian Bows & Arrows...The Old Way by Doug Spotted Eagle	BOO/18	$12.95
❑ Making Arrows...The Old Way by Doug Spotted Eagle	BOO/19	$4.50
❑ Hair of the Bear: Campfire Yarns & Stories by Eric Bye	BOO/20	$9.95
❑ How To Tan Skins The Indian Way by Evard Gibby	BOO/21	$4.95
❑ A Beadwork Companion by Jean Heinbuch	BOO/22	$12.95
❑ Beads and Cabochons by Patricia Lyman	BOO/23	$10.95
❑ Earring Designs by Sig: Book I by Sigrid Wynne-Evans	BOO/24	$10.95
❑ Creative Crafts by Marj by Marj Schneider	BOO/25	$9.95
❑ How To Bead Earrings by Lori Berry	BOO/26	$10.95
❑ Delightful Beaded Earring Designs by Jan Radford	BOO/27	$9.95
❑ Earring Designs by Sig: Book II by Sigrid Wynne-Evans	BOO/28	$10.95
❑ Voices of Native America: Music/Instruments by Doug Spotted Eagle	BOO/29	$17.95
❑ Craft Cord Corral by Janice S. Ackerman	BOO/30	$8.95
❑ Hemp Masters: Hip Hemp Jewelry by Max Lunger	BOO/31	$13.95
❑ Classic Earring Designs by Nola May	BOO/32	$9.95
❑ How To Make Primitive Pottery by Evard Gibby	BOO/33	$8.95
❑ Plains Indian & Mountain Man Arts and Crafts by C. Overstreet	BOO/34	$13.95
❑ Beaded Images: Intricate Beaded Jewelry by Barbara Elbe	BOO/35	$10.95
❑ Earring Designs by Sig-Book III: Celebrations by Sigrid Wynne-Evans	BOO/36	$10.95
❑ Techniques of Fashion Earrings by Deon DeLange	BOO/37	$9.95
❑ Beaded Images II: Intricate Beaded Jewelry by Barbara Elbe	BOO/38	$9.95
❑ Picture Beaded Earrings for Beginners by Starr Steil	BOO/39	$9.95
❑ Plains Indian & Mountain Man Arts and Crafts II by C. Overstreet	BOO/40	$12.95
❑ Simple Lace and Other Beaded Jewelry Patterns by Mary Ellen Harte	BOO/41	$7.95
❑ Beaded Treasure Purses by Deon DeLange	BOO/42	$10.95

EAGLE'S VIEW PUBLISHING READERS SERVICE, DEPT HMGK
6756 North Fork Road - Liberty, Utah 84310

Please send me the above title(s). I am enclosing $_____ (Please add $6.50 per order to cover shipping and handling.) Send check or money order - no cash or C.O.D.s.

Ms./Mrs./Mr. _____

Address _____

City/State/Zip Code _____

Prices and availability subject to change without notice. Allow 2 to 4 weeks for delivery.

HMGK03